JOHN M. ROBERTSON.

The Thinker's Library, No. 50

LETTERS ON REASONING

BY

JOHN M. ROBERTSON

LONDON:

WATTS & CO.,

5 & 6 JOHNSON'S COURT, FLEET STREET, E.C.4

OTHER VOLUMES PUBLISHED IN THIS SERIES

Each bound in clothette, 1s. net

Printed and Published in Great Britain by C. A. Watts & Co. Limited, 5 & 6 Johnson's Court, Fleet Street, London, E.C.4

INTRODUCTION TO THIS ABRIDGED EDITION

THE late J. M. Robertson was a writer whose merits were not so widely or so cordially recognised as they deserved to be. Some such result was doubtless inevitable, since in most of his books Mr. Robertson was an expert writing for a limited circle of fellow experts. He was, moreover, an inveterate champion of unpopular causes ; notably in his theories of Christian origins and in his Shakespearean studies he pursued independent lines of thought with complete indifference to traditional opinions. Under such conditions neither Mr. Robertson himself nor his most ardent admirers could expect that popularity would be achieved.

Nevertheless Mr. Robertson has bequeathed to his fellow-men at least one book which is simple in its language and universal in its appeal. He wrote it for his children—not, as some hasty critics suggested, that they should read it during their childhood, but in order that they should acquire, when they came to confront the great problems of life, an understanding of the mental weapons by which those problems should be attacked. It was Mr. Robertson's conviction that rational thought, sedulously trained and rigorously exercised, was the only sure instrument of wisdom. He had spent much of his time in exposing beliefs based on loose reasoning and emotional prejudices ; he was anxious that his children, in framing their fundamental ideas, should build on sure foundations and on sound logical principles.

Books on logic are supposed to render this service to the mind eager for reasoned convictions. Nevertheless, as Mr. Robertson himself explained, the study of formal logic is both inadequate and beside the mark. In *Letters on Reasoning* logic is made flesh and, instead of a rather uninspiring analysis of abstract processes, becomes a practical gymnastic of the mind. No one can read its pages without feeling a lively stimulus to put his intellectual house in order. They reveal the dangers that haunt every stage in the process of reasoning ; dangers from which the most acute and disciplined minds are never entirely free. The reader may, indeed, derive an added pleasure from the search for instances where Mr. Robertson himself, who was far from claiming infallibility, has diverged from the strait and narrow path of perfect reasoning.

Not the least of the services rendered by these vigorous and challenging *Letters* is that, in expounding the ways of thought, they use as illustrations the search for a solution of the ultimate questions of human destiny. Mr. Robertson helps us to understand why the results of centuries of argument " about it and about " remain unconvincing.

Here, then, is a volume which will be read, and re-read, with interest and profit.

A. G. W.

CONTENTS

vii

LETTER IX

LETTER X

CONTENTS

FROM THE PREFACE TO THE SECOND EDITION

IT seems well to explain here, once for all, that the book is not planned for juvenile readers. The fact of its being addressed to my children has led several reviewers—who, it is interesting to know, cannot have read the first paragraph of the first letter—to observe, not unamiably, that they must be clever children who can understand it. Here the ambiguity of the term "children," although expressly guarded against, has served to illustrate the facility and frequency of wrong inference. As the opening paragraph states, the book was planned to be read by my children when they are grown up : meantime it is meant to help others if it can.

To the more relevant criticisms passed upon it, I have not seen reason to give way in any important matter. One of the canons frequently founded-upon in it was impeached by one reviewer as a fallacy ; but as he vouchsafed no argument I am unable to catch his point of view. Several journals, as was to be expected, complained that I had dealt with religious opinions. Had I supported or founded-on the opinions in question they would not have so complained. So far from admitting that the discussion of such opinions is a fault of method, I have somewhat expanded some of the passages in question. In the belief that such handling of living questions is a good way of vitalising discipline in reasoning, I am more and more encouraged by the movement of academic opinion. Since the issue of the first edition I have had the advantage of reading the instructive work of Mr. Alfred Sidgwick on *The Use of Words in Reasoning* (1901), wherein is temperately maintained and illustrated its author's earlier contention on the inefficacy of formal logic as a means of developing the reasoning powers. Although I cannot wholly acquiesce in his con-clusion that " mistakes in reasoning are nothing but mistakes in the facts from which the reasoning proceeds," I can cordially assent to his judgment that " our modern errors have a pedigree ; and Logic will remain an almost useless study so long as we forget that it is in the subject-matter of reasoning, not in any abstract ' reasoning-process,' that all effective error is concealed." The more need to grapple, in such a treatise as the present, with some of the more vital errors known to be current. I might even claim, I think, the ratification of a sentence of Professor Bradley, who has written :

For myself, though I have not hesitated to point out the falsity and immorality of some Christian doctrines (where this seemed necessary), I cannot approve of the widespread practice of treating them as devoid even of existence— [1]

though I baulk at the phrasing of the last clause. Un-fortunately, while an academic writer such as Green may turn his function to the account of his religious beliefs, academic writers who do not agree with him are debarred from confuting him in treatises meant for the use of students. One can but hope that ere long the education of the reasoning faculty will be generally gone about by way of a real gymnastic in at least non-religious discussion of real problems. But as regards re-ligious problems we are bound to say, with Mr. Sidgwick (p. 39), that " In the general ignorance of Logic which prevails, and which is fostered by the traditional teaching system, it is not difficult to make people accept a circular truism as a deep philosophical truth." I have taken some pains to expose one such process.

March, 1905.

---

[1] *Appearance and Reality*, 3rd ed., App., p. 558.

LETTERS ON REASONING

LETTER I

My Dear Children,

I sometimes wonder whether, when you grow up, you will care enough about any of my studies to wish to read what I wrote about them. It is not at all likely that either of you will care enough about *all* of them to read all my books; and I can neither guess what choice either of you may make, nor decide how I would like to have you choose. But when I think of you growing up and forming your minds, perhaps after I am dead, there comes to me a wish that at that stage you should have at least one book of mine which I may ask you to read for your own sake and for mine, whatever your mental tastes may be. If I should be gone when you become old enough to understand these letters, you will read them none the less willingly because, while written for you, they may have served also for other young people.

There is a fair chance that you may both turn out less fond of reading than I was; and I have no great wish that you should grow up to write books. There are so many already; and it is so hard to write a good one. When I look into the earlier of my own, I always wince over something, and wish I could rewrite them; and in the margins of the later and larger I often make additions, to improve them. There are many other ways of using the mind and the eyesight that are at least quite as pleasure-giving and quite as useful. What I *would* counsel you to do is to live your lives cordially and joyously, never shunning serious matters because they are serious, but living, so to speak, much in the sunshine. Partake freely of great music and great art;

think about them all you can ; and read—so I advise, whatever may be your bias—plenty of poetry and good fiction, taking what guidance you can get from people and writers who seem to you intelligent, but always trying to judge for yourselves what you have read.

There is, however, little need thus to counsel you to range freely in imaginative literature : we all seem to take to that very readily, whether or not we read critically. More necessary is it to urge people to read a good deal of history ; and this I trust you will both do, as I cannot see how mankind is ever to grow collectively wiser until it has learned from the errors and successes of past generations how to escape their failures and provide for a steadier progress. But I am not going to make these letters a guide-book to your studies in general. Such a guide-book, even if better done than I can do it, might be profitably superseded in ten years' time by a new manual, telling of new books. What I want to do is to leave you some suggestions which I think may be of use to you whatever your other studies or pursuits may be.

I am not concerned to think of you as experts in any one science (though it is well worth while to be that), or in philology, or in archæology, or even in music, or Greek, or Shakespeare. A clever logician, Professor de Morgan, has well said that it is good to know everything of something, and something of everything ; and though I agree with him (it being understood, of course, that such counsels of perfection can never be fulfilled), I shall not try to choose your something for you. But whether you lean towards the second or towards the first of those splendid impossibles, I trust you will both be good reasoners. I want you, Guenn, as well as you, Guy, to regard this as specially well worth your while. If I read your little " bumps " aright, you will not be equally devoted to study ; but in so far as our reasoning powers *can* be improved by exercise and discipline, there is no good reason why women should not undergo it as well as men, and as successfully.

When you grow up there will still, I fear, be people who think that a woman should not be reasonable : indeed, you are both likely to hear it said that " reason " is a " cold " or otherwise repellent faculty, which needs checking rather than encouraging. Such sayings are their own sufficient refutation. If you will weigh them with me, you will have taken one practical step in reasoning.

Only the other day I heard an educated man argue that much harm had been done in politics by the cultivation of and the appeal to reason. When it was suggested to him that his own remark was meant to be a piece of reasoning, an appeal to reason, he sought to make his case clearer by saying he meant " logic " ; and when asked whether he did not want to be logical he said he had in view " formal logic," and that by formal logic he understood an entire disregard of feeling and emotion. This was all a verbal confusion on his own part. " Formal logic " is a well-understood term for a quasi-mathematical or algebraic way of handling questions of abstract logic, which never arise in political discussion at all. This was not what was in his mind. What he ought to have said, to express his own thought, was that harm may be done in politics by assuming, what is not true, that men in the mass are able to appreciate and to apply a highly reasonable system of government. A thinker who frames a theory of government on grounds of abstract justice is certainly " appealing to reason " ; but it is not " reason " or good reasoning that makes him overlook the incapacity of many men to live justly by the light of reason. In forgetting to take such a fact into account he has failed to reason with due care. To realise his oversight is an act of reason. Unfortunately some, in vaguely realising the oversight, fall into the worse absurdity of saying that we had better reason less.

That very remark is a blundering appeal to reason. All argument, every attempt to influence opinion or conduct by presenting a " because," is a process of reasoning. In studying religious questions you are likely to read, or to hear, the kind of protest I have just glanced at ; and if you have not learned to think clearly you may be confused by it. Great writers—and many who are not great—have given forth the bad sophism that since our reason is fallible, since we are liable to make mistakes, we should cease to reason. As if that

very formula were not simply a self-confounding appeal
to reason, an attempt to persuade by a " because."
If we were really convinced that our judgment—which
is only another way of naming our reason—is quite
untrustworthy, we should have reached that very conclusion (which, if convinced, we should *trust*) by reasoning; and if we should then propose either to stop
judging altogether or to accept thenceforth whatever
any particular teacher might tell us, we should only
stultify ourselves; for to decide to stop judging is to
judge that we ought to stop, and to accept another's
judgment is to judge that it is acceptable.

I deal with this verbal problem at the outset of these
letters because it is typical of many of the confusions
that will meet you even in argumentative literature, to
say nothing of ordinary table-talk. One of the most
pretentious of the serious books published in my time
—Mr. Benjamin Kidd's *Social Evolution*—is a systematic
application of the absurd species of argument we have
been considering. He says to his readers, in effect : " I
reason thus : reasoning (= reason) is a dangerous guide :
let us then reasonably decide not to be reasonable, and
so by reasoning escape the evil consequences of all
reasoning." And his book has had a great sale, for
the " reason " that it flatters the folly of many religious
people who like to hear " reason " disparaged.

Seeing that such books still gratify many educated
people, I cannot hope that when you are growing to
maturity their ideas will not come in your way. What
I wish is that you shall be able to judge them intelligently, and to dismiss them with decision. I want you
therefore to grasp first the truth that *all* attempts to
persuade are processes of reasoning. Some, we say, are
good or " logical " or " valid " ; by which we mean
that on analysis their parts or stages are consistent. A
good reasoner is one who does not contradict himself
in the course of his argument, and who further takes
intelligent account of all the important facts of the case
he is dealing with. A " bad reasoner " is one who, in
seeking to prove or to convince, takes up (like Mr.
Kidd) contradictory positions, whether or not he has the
main facts of his case before him. It is probable that
the difference between a very bad and a very good

reasoner is on a par with that between an ugly and a beautiful person, or that between a "colour-blind" person and one of normal vision—something irreparable, something fundamentally unalterable. Happily, however, there are countless degrees between extreme ugliness and perfect loveliness, and utter uncomeliness is as rare as flawless beauty. And as the plain face may become lovely in virtue of goodness looking from the eyes, or be pleasing through its perfect health, so a mind little gifted with quickness or clearness of insight may through candour and careful exercise become competent for all the normal tasks of judgment.

To fail of such competence, and yet to put forth judgments freely in daily intercourse, is to be a nuisance to more intelligent people, though the incompetent pass muster well enough in each other's society—until, that is, they dispute over some question which stirs their passions. Then they are apt to disesteem each other with virulence. In ordinary society, there is ready and severe criticism of slovenliness in dress, unpleasant habits, ill-breeding in the matter of small talk or offensive gossip, or an uneducated pronunciation ; but for incoherent reasoning as such there is the tolerance of a common laxity. I want you nevertheless to take as much care about your opinions as about your clothes and your bodies and your manners, and so to be fit for the true "good society," that of cultured and thoughtful men and women.

It is, of course, part of the law of mutual forbearance that we should bear with bad reasoning when it meets us in intercourse, especially if it come from unaffectedly unwise persons. But if we think long and seriously about human affairs we can hardly fail to see that endless evil comes of the failure of most people even to aim at consistency in thought and action. Consistency in thought is the gist of right thinking, of good reasoning ; and consistency in action is the gist of right conduct. All reasoning, all morality works down to that test ; and all deflection from reasonableness and righteousness may be expressed in terms of inconsistency. Now, conduct depends finally upon thought, and it seems clear that, though a habit of reasoning soundly on non-moral problems will not necessarily develop scrupulous thinking on

moral problems, the habit of aiming at consistency in
one's reasoning in general will help one to check inconsistency in one's practice when one is concerned to
do so.

On the other hand, it is hard to conceive that a
habitually slovenly or inconsistent reasoner can be highly
consistent in conduct, though he keep strictly within the
bounds of criminal law.   It is quite true that a not very
clear-headed person may have strong sympathetic or
unselfish instincts, while a clear-headed one may not ;
but if the former is habitually consistent in normal conduct it must be because on that side he *is* clear-headed,
or at least anxiously reflective, and it is historically
certain that normally conscientious people may, for lack
of the habit of consistent reasoning, act with gross inconsistency in a new relation, where moral habit does not
guide them.   The naturally selfish or unsympathetic
person, again, cannot be made worse by the habit of
scrupulous reasoning, and he may be very much improved
by it on the moral side.   I take it, then, that to be a
good reasoner is a duty only less pressing than that of
being a good citizen, a good man or woman ; and my
ideal for you is that you should so regard the intellectual
life.

All honourable people, I suppose, realise that to act
rightly we must habitually seek consistency : the law
of " doing as we would be done by " is the normal
summary of the moral code.   Yet even of those who
avowedly accept that code, many are lax in applying
it ; and this I suspect to be explicable in terms of the
fact that it is comparatively rare to realise at all the
bearing of the principle of consistency on processes of
thought.   You see I say " explicable in terms of " rather
than " due to," because I do not wish to prejudge here
the question whether it is a moral impulse that moves
us to reason more scientifically or a logical perception
of inconsistency that moves us to be more honest.   That
is a very interesting problem, whether you consider it
as one of metaphysics or as one of psychology ; and I
hope you will be able to take an interest in metaphysics
and psychology, were it only to fit you to defend yourselves against bad metaphysicians.   But I do not want
to load these letters with special problems : I want

to help you, if I can, to develop your general powers of judgment by way of the exercise of reasoning. And as I have a conviction that, in respect of certain natural tendencies which hinder us, we all have more or less difficulty in realising the need for consistency in our reasoning processes, I wish to stress the importance of the connection between the so-called " intellectual " and the moral processes.

To me it serves as a measure of both the moral and the intellectual shortcomings of mankind, thus far, that intellectual consistency is so little regarded. I should put it that such inconsistency is *intellectual immorality* ; and I can hope for you nothing better than that you may find yourselves at middle life in a world in which such immorality is more clearly realised and more seriously resisted than it is in my day. In that case you will live among better and wiser people, generally speaking, than your predecessors.

You see, then, that in begging you to be thoughtful and careful reasoners I am urging on you not a mere intellectual gymnastic, much less a habit of quibbling and wanton disputation, but a vital self-culture that shall evolve and elevate your personalities. I am not prescribing, you will find, a study of logic in the technical sense of that term. I do indeed hope that, whether before or after you read these letters, you will study some treatises on logic. The works of such men as John Mill, Professor Bain, Professor Minto, and Mr. Bradley are full of instructive thought as well as of gymnastic discipline. But logic is the name we give to the body of analysis of the process of reasoning in general, and is rather a general formulation of the rules of all proof and reasoned belief than a training in correct reasoning. Technical logic is to actual reasoning very much what grammar is to language : that is to say, its rules are abstracted from study of the processes of careful and tested reasoning, as grammar is primarily a statement of rules seen to prevail in the speech of educated people. And as the way we learn to speak and write correctly is just by speaking as educated people speak and write, with formulated grammar to remind us and to fix our memories, so the way we learn to reason correctly is by following or checking arguments, with logic to fix for us in condensed forms our recognition of the nature of all processes of argument.

If you should learn any foreign language from books, you will find that even to get by heart the rules of its grammar is a very imperfect way of mastering grammatical speech, as compared with the method of following actual speech and written style. So I believe it to be with logic, in the technical sense. Of course we often use the term logic to signify simply consistent reasoning, and the term logical to signify "coherent, consistent, reasonable." In that sense I want you to be logical for the reasons I have already given. Those who disparage logicality in this sense are either thoughtful but confused people who fall into fallacy like the reasoner I mentioned above, or people ill-fitted for thinking. To despise or to fear logicality of mind is as foolish or mistaken as to despise or fear truthfulness.

But even in the technical sense of the term, remember, logic is not an ignoring or stunting of the processes or forces of emotion and imagination. Many common phrases on the subject are bad fallacies. When Macaulay in his History remarks that "Logic admits of no compromise: the essence of politics is compromise: it is therefore not strange that some of the most important and most useful political instruments in the world should be among the most illogical compositions that ever were penned," he is creating a confusion similar to that I have discussed above. To say that logic does not admit of compromise is about as useful as to say that it does not admit of bicycling or making love. Compromise is an action or an agreement to act. Logic, as I have said, is the analysis and correct statement of the processes of proof—proof of propositions. Now, in a legal document, such as a deed of sale, a declaration of the change or establishment of a dynasty, or a will, we are not dealing with a process of proof: we are setting forth an agreement of certain persons to act in a given way, or a stipulation that certain persons, specially appointed, shall do certain things. If, accordingly, a testator disposes of his property in a way that we think foolish, his will is not therefore to be described as illogical. If it secures its end, it is practically "logical."

So with a parliamentary declaration. What Macaulay

had in view was the declaration of the English Parliament declaring the throne vacant after the revolution of 1688 : a statement embodying the various grounds on which different politicians were willing to make a change in the monarchy. Now, the " logical " course in such a matter was just to set forth these grounds in such a way as to secure the great majority of votes : the question was not one of proving a truth, but one of getting men to pledge themselves to a certain course, to enact a certain law. The framers of the resolution would have been " illogical " indeed if they had so framed it that it was offensive to the majority. They were " logical " in the sense that they carried out their practical purpose in a prudent way. Macaulay is talking at random when he says : " They cared little whether their major agreed with their conclusion, if the major secured two hundred votes, and the conclusion two hundred more." There was no major, no minor, and no syllogistic conclusion in the matter ; they were not maintaining a proposition in the logical sense of the phrase ; they were drawing up a " motion to be carried." For them, the sole " proposition to be proved " was this : " We shall best carry our point—the crowning of William—by moving a resolution formally expressing the reasons for which the largest number of members of the legislature are willing to crown him." Of such a proposition the desired " proof " could be given only by the actual voting. The business in hand was not to prove a truth, but to please a number of men, and forecast their action.

To call the document " illogical " is merely to show misconception of what " logic " means. If you will read the arguments of Lord Somers on the *wording* of the resolution, you will see that he was a very clear and logical—that is, a consistent—reasoner ; and his reasonings may be reduced to a series of syllogisms by anyone who cares to take the trouble. Macaulay himself glimpsed the nature of the case when, after citing the phrases incriminating the deposed king, he wrote : " Such words are to be considered, not as words, but as deeds." Quite so—though it would be better to read " not as arguments " : they are not an attempt to prove an assertion ; they are the avowal of an agreement as to a line of action ; and it is a gratuitous sophism to say of them, " they are rational though they may be contradictory." They are not contradictory. The current theory of the British monarchy is no doubt illogical in the sense of being inconsistent and incoherent. It is easy to show that men hold by monarchy either because they are themselves unreasonable or because they distrust the capacity of their fellows to act justly and reasonably in politics beyond a certain point. It would not be hard to prove that those men are either illogical or insincere who profess to believe in the indefeasible right of a community to choose its rulers and also in the indefeasible right of monarchs to rule through hereditary descent. Broadly speaking, the English nation in 1688 was mainly made up of muddle-headed people. It is so now. But it does not follow that the formula in question is a contradiction in terms, or even that it contradicted the (unreasonable) standing principle that the blame for the king's errors lies on his counsellors, or even that it was framed by muddle-headed or superstitious men. It may have been framed by men who were themselves above the monarchic superstition, and capable of living judiciously under a republican system, but convinced of the need for humouring and managing most of their superstitious fellow-citizens by means of arbitrary compromises between monarchy and self-government.

The phenomena or forces of emotion and imagination may as well as any other forces be subject-matter of logical propositions ; and if, in any argument which claims to trace and explain a process of social or personal causation, the actual play of emotion and imagination in all such processes be overlooked, the argument is so far fallacious. Further, a logical mind may easily be more emotional and imaginative than an illogical. The love of truth and rectitude *is* an emotion ; the recognition of a good argument is a solidly pleasurable feeling ; and it is an observable fact that the habit of self-criticism, to the end of attaining consistency, can expand imagination by widening sympathy. People who cannot think in an orderly way are fain to suppose themselves more imaginative than others ; but though some kinds of imagination may flourish in the inverse ratio of the usage of consistent reasoning, some of the highest kinds of all actually arise from it.

It is a bad mistake to credit great " imagination " to peasants who explain puzzling facts by stories of fairies and fiends, and to deny it to the mathematic mind of Newton, " voyaging through strange seas of thought alone." Never, I beg you, let yourselves be browbeaten by people who tell you that to cultivate your reason is to lose the faculty for enjoying poetry, music, or any other art. The truth lies the other way. Exercise of the reason may indeed raise you above some kinds of enjoyment that appealed to your untrained mind, but it will rather enlarge your faculty for enjoying greater art, by widening, so to speak, the range of the vibration of your feelings.

This, of course, holds true of many forms of special study as well as of the habitual use of the reflective reason, because every study involves processes of reasoning. But I have often observed that the study of a special subject or science may leave a man awkward in the use of his reason on other subjects, even those which more or less obviously concern all of us. And it is because, in particular, I do not think manuals of logic the best exercises for developing the reasoning powers that I have set about writing these letters. The late Mr. Jevons tells, in the preface to his *Studies in Deductive Logic*, that he has " often been astonished at the way in which even well-trained students," prepared only by mathematics, " break down before a simple logical problem. A man who is very ready at integration begins to hesitate and flounder when he is asked such a simple question as the following : ' If all triangles are plane figures, what information, if any, does this proposition give us concerning things which are not triangles ? ' " I readily accept Mr. Jevons's testimony as to the insufficiency of mathematics to make us good reasoners in other fields of thought ; but I doubt whether the kind of inefficiency of which he has given a sample would not be more easily cured by general exercise in reasoning *followed* by a study of logic, than by making logical exercises a primary means of training the reason. An athlete, I suspect, can better be trained by free exercise in play, followed by special gymnastic, than by

taking him with undeveloped physique and setting him
at once to special exercises.

In my copy of Mr. Jevons's *Studies*, bought at second-
hand, some previous reader had written in pencil, under
the passage above quoted, these words : " Some plane
figures are not triangles." That is *his* answer to the
question which Mr. Jevons says has puzzled clever mathematical students. Now, you will see that this answer is
a blunder. The proposition cited in the question above
quoted gives *no* information as to things which are not
triangles. No doubt, if you heard such a proposition
you might, without any further information about plane
figures, surmise that things not triangles could also be
plane figures ; but you do not get that fact as information from the proposition under notice. The pencilled
answer I have quoted happens to be a true proposition ;
but it is not here a properly drawn logical inference.

Technical or deductive logic, you will observe, deals
thus strictly with the content of propositions, taking
no account of merely possible implications ; and as Mr.
Minto remarks, " nothing has contributed more to bring
upon it the reproach of quibbling." I do not for a
moment join in that reproach. The resort to quibbling
should bring reproach not on the exactitude of strict
logic, but on the person who turns it to the account
of quibbling. But, inasmuch as the exercises of technical
logic involve much artificial verbal distinguishment, reduced to symbolic unreality, I doubt whether they
prepare our minds to draw the material distinctions
which are of the essence of right thinking in regard to
the living problems of belief and action. On the other
hand, the free use, so to speak, of your limbs in living
reasoning will prepare you as well as may be for the
small feats of technical logic, which discipline you can
undergo all the more easily when so prepared.

To return, finally, to the question of the value of good
habits of reasoning. I would have you realise very
clearly that all discussion, all criticism, whether wise or
unwise, *is* reasoning. The blunderers who warn you
against reason are simply bad or temporarily confused
reasoners. There is no getting away from reasoning,
save by way of insanity ; and insanity itself simulates
the process of reasoning. The common use of the word

" irrational " is thus lax, though convenient. We may indeed fitly describe as irrationalists the people who cry down reason ; but their fallacy is none the less an attempt to reason. Still more clearly do those appeal to reason who warn you that " man does not live by reason alone," or that close devotion to processes of reasoning may weaken the emotional and imaginative side of your nature.

Such warnings, as they stand, are simply counsels of mental hygiene. No one ever disputed that in order to live a full and rounded life we should cultivate our æsthetic faculties, the life of the eye and ear and the conscience and the imagination. Travel and living observation and friendly intercourse are all capital elements in a cultured life ; and poetry is as it were the flower of all literature, all experience. But the givers of such counsels, when they begin to disparage reason, are themselves doing on that side what they warn you against doing on the other. Too often they have cultivated only the æsthetic faculties ; and we find them disposing of the deepest intellectual problems by purely æsthetic tests, applauding a fallacious theory or a false narrative merely because it pleases their imagination or comforts their feelings. Disparaging reason, they are really perverting and corrupting it in their own case. Such fallacy-mongers are sometimes very amiable and charming people ; but in the intellectual life, as I have already put it, they are nuisances, by reason of the ignorant confidence with which they darken counsel.

It would mortify me to believe that you will grow up members of that fallacious tribe. You, my dear Guenn, must not let yourself feel that because at any time social usage or your immediate circle does not urge you to use your brains scrupulously you do well to be satisfied with hand-to-mouth thinking. I hope that you will never be swayed by the judgments of either men or women who do not like that a woman should be wise or instructed. Your tact, I trust, will always save you from being pedantic, or from obtruding unseasonably the process of reasoning. But you, my dear Guy, owe just the same consideration to the laws of pleasant intercourse : tact and adaptability should not be left to women any more than sound and scrupulous reasoning should be left to men.   It pleases me to hope that you will so grow up as to be comrades both socially and intellectually ; that if either of you lags mentally the other will encourage and help, and that if either tends to be lacking in tact or amenity the other will affectionately admonish.

LETTER II

In the previous letter I remarked that a careful process of reasoning may be left practically useless or misleading because of the reasoner's failure to note some essential facts or data. It would not, perhaps, be too much to say that the majority of men's errors of opinion proceed rather from wrong or insufficient information than from fallacy of inference. When I reflect on the nature of great masses of the didactic literature of the past, now admittedly superseded, it seems to me to wear a certain uniform air of confidence in error ; and while the confidence has to be set down as the besetting sin of humanity, the error comes at least as often from wrong testimony, traditional or otherwise, as from illicit reasoning. Education of the reason, then, is likely to involve no less a vigilant scrutiny of testimony than a scrupulous regard to inference.

I cannot, indeed, too strongly press upon you the importance of being slow to believe where your decision will have any width of bearing. Here again you will be met by loud protests from a certain order of minds. Doubt, you will often be told, is something " cold " and " dark." I do not much value argument by metaphor ; but it might perhaps benefit such metaphor-mongers to ask themselves whether in the order of nature we are not daily refreshed by darkness and yearly braced by cold. It would not be unjust, I think, to say of them that their fear of the " cold " is like that of the nerveless bather who recoils from the plunge, and their fear of the " dark " like that felt by or instilled into many children—I say " instilled into," because in your own case your mother and I have thus far succeeded in preventing its being suggested to you, and neither of you has ever shown the slightest sign of feeling it. In the old fashion I would say, May this be a good omen.

The censure of doubt is in fact only an aspect of the censure of reason ; for doubt is the beginning of reason. In other words, it is the beginning of wisdom. If I were bent on meeting *a priori* speculations with *a priori* speculations, I could make some play, I think, with the formula that, since the whole of intellectual evolution as we know it is through doubt, the " purpose " of the process seems to be to evoke doubt. Consider the myriads of animals that must have perished for lack of doubt about the fitness of certain things for food, the safeness of certain places, the possible nearness of dangerous enemies. Most animals, I should say, are now doubters upon instinct, their species having survived by dint of doubting. The trout passing the hook ; the horse swerving from a strange object ; the sheep, even in captivity, scurrying from one who approaches them ; the mouse darting towards its hole at a sound ; the dog barking at a strange footstep ; the deer flying at the scent of some possible enemy far away—do they not all exemplify an " economy of doubt " in nature ?

As for man, every step he has made in civilisation has been taken in virtue of either doubt or the doubt-involving substitution of a new belief for an old ; and every such step, depend upon it, has been resisted by experienced people who denounced criticism as their type to-day denounces doubt and reason. It has always been common for theologians to denounce, not merely wrong belief, but " unbelief." We shall consider in another letter the temper in which they speak : let us here note their formal inconsistency—their want of logic. They themselves are just as much " unbelievers " as anybody else. Their creed took its rise by way of disbelief in another creed ; their first teachers were unbelievers. Right and wrong beliefs alike involve disbelief ; every new religion negates in whole or in part previous religions ; and the process from one belief to another which negates it is either an insane spasm of emotion or a process of doubt.

Each believer in turn disbelieves the doctrine which contradicts him ; and just as the Christians spoke of the " unbelieving Moslems," so the Moslems spoke of the " infidel Christians." To-day the religionist who denounces " unbelief " is an unbeliever in the Naturalism

which rejects his faith ; and in every generation the
so-called " believers " have been the most obstinate unbelievers in new truth. When they are on the way to a
reluctant assimilation of some of the truths which they
and their predecessors had denied, they are doubters.

It is implied in all this that we need to be on our
guard against errors both of credulity and of incredulity ;
but inasmuch as uncritical belief to start with commits
us in a measure to disbelief in new lore which contradicts
that already held, it is on the side of over-ready confidence that the stress of danger lies. I have advised
you to repel the self-stultifying counsel " Do not trust
to reason," but I urge you strongly " Do not lightly
trust to statements of fact." Guard against the risks
of wrong reasoning, not by reasoning less, but by reasoning more. That is, demand evidence or argument not
merely for new doctrine, but for old. The kind of
thinker who denounces " unbelief " is himself extremely
hard of belief in the new doctrine ; but the intelligently
rational course is to be equally critical of all. As Professor Bain insists, there is in our nature a primary
and powerful bent to credulity ; but with the growth of
reason there is evolved an equally powerful tendency
to reject whatever clearly contradicts the belief in possession. The first belief blocks the way ; and to cure
this evil we had need acquire, first, the habit of enquiring
before we believe to begin with ; and secondly a willing-
ness to reconsider, on challenge, even a belief taken up
after investigation. And such habits are hard to set
up. Mankind has learned to doubt even as it has learned
to follow the sequences of nature, to control forces, to
heal diseases, to manage social affairs. The faculty for
doubt develops with the range of knowledge ; and it is
still the general rule that where we have imperfect
knowledge we tend to believe too readily unless our
previous beliefs clearly negate the proposition in question.

Let me give you some instances. Professor Minto,
one of the logicians I have praised above, early won my
admiration by the sagacity with which in his writings
he detected current errors of statement or narrative on
various subjects which he had to investigate. His book
on *Logic : Deductive and Inductive* is, I think, the best
introduction you could have to technical logic, so lucid

is it, so fresh and alive in its handling. But now and then, though as I have said he had a gift for investigation, even he is unduly compliant in his acceptance of statements of historic fact. Thus, writing about " the coincidence that has been remarked between race and different forms of Christianity in Europe," he says :

" If the distribution of systems were entirely independent of race, it might be said that you would expect one system to coincide equally often with different races in proportion to the positive number of their communities. But the Greek system is found almost solely among Slavonic peoples, the Roman among the Celtic, and the Protestant among Teutonic. *The coincidence is greater than chance will account for.* Is the explanation then to be found in some special adaptability of the religious system to the character of the people ? This may be the right explanation, but we have not proved it by merely discounting chance. To prove this we must show that there was no other cause at work ; that character was the only operative condition in the choice of system ; that political combinations, for example, had nothing to do with it. The presumption from extra-casual coincidence is only that there is a special cause : in determining what that is, we must conform to the ordinary conditions of explanation." [1]

Here, in the very act of ostensibly warning us against a too hasty inference, Mr. Minto has actually made that inference, and his warning is consequently a contradiction in terms. And the whole miscarriage, I think, has arisen through his too ready acceptance of a wrong statement of fact. The important point for us at present is this mistaken acceptance ; but if you will take the trouble to follow with me the miscarriage in the argument you will perhaps realise more vividly how important the factual error is.

I have italicised, you see, the sentence about the coincidence being greater than chance will account for. Now, that is, to begin with, an oddly loose phrase for Mr. Minto. It is strictly meaningless to say that chance can " account for " anything. Chance, as I shall try to show at length in another letter, is the name we give to *untraced or untraceable causation of events or coincidences*. It will here suffice, however, to note that while Mr. Minto in effect says : " These coincidences of phenomena are so nearly invariable that there *must be* a causal connection between them "—that is, between race and racial creed—he yet goes on to say, in effect, that

[1] Work cited, pp. 359, 360.

" political combinations " *might* conceivably have some-thing " to do with " the distribution of creeds on racial lines. Then, unless the name " political combinations " includes the idea of " race character " (in which case both phrases are reduced to insignificance), it follows that there may be no causal connection whatever between race and creed.

The confusion is complete, and I think we can trace it all to the acceptance of the error of fact. Religion and race do *not* coincide, as is alleged. 1. The Greek system is not confined to Slavonic peoples : the Greeks even now are certainly not all Slavonic ; and some " Slavonic " populations either never were or have ceased to be Greek Christians. 2. The Roman system flourishes to-day in great sections of the German-speaking peoples, who pass for " Teutonic " ; also in various Teutonic cantons of Switzerland, including the oldest ; also among Flemings, who equally rank as Teutonic. 3. The Protestant sys-tem flourishes among the " Celtic " peoples of the Scotch Highlands, Wales, and Cornwall ; it prevails in several French-speaking cantons of Switzerland ; and it did live vigorously for generations in France. If the people of France and French-speaking Switzerland are not to be reckoned as " Celtic," then many of them are—in the terms of the division subsumed—Roman Catholic Teutons.

I do not here concern myself with the question as to what races are properly to be called Celtic or Teutonic, and why : on that problem, as well as on the racial distribution of Catholicism and Protestantism, I have written at length in other books. I simply proceed on Mr. Minto's own terminology and classification. Taking these for granted, we find that he is astray in his facts : there is a very frequent crossing of the lines of race and creed. And it was probably a suspicion of his own error that led him to go on to suggest that political combinations may have determined the distribution of church systems. This, I have elsewhere undertaken to show, is really the case. Yet, not having eradicated his historical error, he leaves standing, in his sentence about chance, the theorem usually bracketed with that error. (I say bracketed with, because I suspect that the theorem partly preceded the formulated error ; men reasoning

B

thus : " I, a Teuton, am Protestant ; he, a Celt, is
Catholic ; doubtless all Teutons are Protestants, and all
Celts Catholics ; indeed, such is the fact.") Finally, he
is committed to suggesting that what he affirms to
be an evidently causal coincidence between race and
church-system may not be such a coincidence at all.
Had he with sufficient energy doubted the pseudo-
historical statement, the train of confused reasoning
would not have arisen.[1]

Now, if such a man as Mr. Minto could thus miscarry,
you and I may be pretty sure that we can.   Seeking
to be on our guard, we may ask ourselves whether he
was originally misled by force of a survival of either
religious or racial bias ; whether, that is, he held himself
for a " Teuton," and reckoned Protestantism a superior
form of church polity to Catholicism—as he possibly
might, even after ceasing to be a churchman at all.   On
that hypothesis we shall presumably do well to ask ourselves, when we are disposed to accept without anxious
investigation any important generalisation, whether it
flatters in any way whatever our self-esteem.

I recall a similar case of historical error on the part of
another very able man—the late Professor W. K. Clifford.
That brilliant thinker has asserted that " the Teutonic
conscience protested in the Reformation " against the
reference of right and wrong to the arbitrary will of
deity as a standard.[2]   In this passage the Professor is
seeking to build up a rational moral standard which
shall be more scrupulous than others ; and in his essay
on " The Ethics of Belief " he becomes still more stringent in his prescriptions for the intellectual life.   Again
and again he insists on the harm done by accepting
current assertions without strict examination, on the
danger to society of such careless credulity, on the sacred
obligation of enquiry before belief.   Well, in the passage
above cited he has without any enquiry echoed and
endorsed a vulgar error ; an error, too, which specially
merits his own censure in that it ministers to racial pride

---

[1] I ought to note that Professor Minto had completed his book
on Logic only a short time before his death, and after years of
worsening ill-health.
[2] Essay on " Right and Wrong," in *Lectures and Essays*, ed. 1886,
p. 335.

and malice. There was nothing specially " Teutonic "
in the revolt of " conscience " against false morals at the
Reformation : such a revolt had been made a hundred
times before by non-Teutons ; and if we closely study
the history of the Reformation we shall find that it
took rather more " conscientious " lines in France than
in Germany ; the German movement being, by the
admission of Luther, in many respects far from conscientious. Nay, Luther himself actually framed a theological doctrine of morals which realises the very conception that Professor Clifford denounces ; and the
" Teutonic " Locke, in ascribing the nature of right
and wrong to divine volition, did the same thing with a
difference.

Thus our moralist has been careless where he incul-
cates care ; and his carelessness certainly justifies his
own warning, for by endorsing that falsism about the
" Teutonic conscience " he encourages those of his readers
who suppose themselves Teutons to believe that they
have a better sort of conscience than members of other
races, and to look on other races, accordingly, through
a perverting conceit, which easily evolves a pernicious
ill-will. Once more, if such an acute and original thinker
can fall into such inconsistency, all through an un-
thinking acceptance of a familiar formula, you and I
may so err. Let me urge on you then to form the habit,
which has only very gradually become normal with me,
of asking yourself, over every such use of a far-reaching
generalisation, whether it stands for tested knowledge,
whether it is not merely a shibboleth of national or
racial vanity, or at least an imperfect formulation of a
complex mass of facts, caught at by most people as a
labour-saving expression.

Science progresses by the scrutiny of such imperfect
formulas at the hands of men who have the scrutinising
instinct or habit, or who happen in a special case to
have been luckily sceptical. But I have noticed that
men trained in the physical sciences are very prone to
accept without question the imperfect formulas of the
moral sciences ; and you see how Clifford, even in an
original investigation of ethics, thoughtlessly accepted a
claptrap formula from history.

My words imply, however, that even in their own

fields many specialists are fixed in false formulas. The claptrap historical formula came from historians ; the new theory in physics or biology has to fight the experts in possession, who stand by the old. This is one of the most familiar phenomena in the history of culture ; and yet men are surprisingly slow to act warily on the knowledge. I have long had the suspicion that if for a single year the specialists in every field of thought would systematically doubt and challenge every one of their current generalisations, taking nothing for granted, there would be stirring times in the way of new truth.

In my own intellectual pilgrimage every special investigation, I think I may say, has led me to revise some of the conclusions I have found current even among " experts." In such various fields as political economy, mythology, Christian origins, the philosophy of history, psychology, the study of Shakespeare, the analysis of verse, the criticism of literature and men of letters, I seem to myself to find some errors accepted, some truths missed, some traditional judgments blocking the way. It was not that I set out expecting such an experience : I simply wanted, I think, to understand, to realise how things had gone : the general doubt emerges from the experience. And when I reflect how unleisured has been much of my own research, how much has been made by the midnight lamp, how ill-equipped have often been my expeditions, I can easily conceive that even if I have not been wholly astray in my innovating conclusions, my formulas will soon need recasting, my survey fresh adjustments. If either of you should ever follow any of my trails, I beg you to aim at correcting my views ; it ought to be no hard matter, in your day, if you take fair pains.

In any case, remember that, whatever views you set out with, whatever beliefs you have in stock in youth, you probably hold some of them over-confidently ; some of them will probably turn out to be wrong. Try, therefore, to look critically at every fact or set of data on which you found an argument or a conviction. I mean, of course, in the way of serious study and important action. One must guard against overdoing doubt in normal intercourse : table-talk will not bear the strain of either the Socratic or the scientific method ;

and it is unamiable, not to say clownish, habitually to obtrude distrust. But it is well to have comrades who do not dislike doubt, whether by way of jest or of earnest. As Emerson says, the truly well-bred people (or let us say the well-educated people) are those who are not easily shocked—shocked, that is, by serious challenges to their beliefs.

It may seem to you, on reading thus far, as if I were urging you to pass your lives in a state of hesitation. Rather I am seeking to save you, by a discipline in doubt, from the most painful kind of hesitations, those which come to us when we are forced in our own despite to ask whether we have not on some great issue been working injustice, whether we have not been long on the wrong side. If such a doubt is ever forced upon you, I trust you will find it painful. Many people, I confess, seem not to be made unhappy by it. They forgive themselves for injustice as readily as they commit it, as easily as they have credited untruth. I hope you will not be of that order of moralists. I can conceive no more painful intellectual experience than the discovery that we have stoned a true prophet, resisted a true doctrine, backed an injustice. People are always doing these things for lack of due doubt ; and there is small profit in the discovery if it do not warn us against fresh blunders.

Religious people, I notice, speak much of the pain caused to them and their like by attacks on their beliefs ; they say little of any pain they have felt on finding that they had denounced the bringer of a new truth. Now, every challenge to an opinion which we hold warmly or emotionally is likely to be at least annoying. I can remember well how in my teens I was hurt or angered by some criticisms of my literary heroes which I learned later to regard as substantially just. I therefore advise you, when you are so hurt or angered, to think a long while before you condemn the critic. The effort will reward you. You will not always find, after careful study, that you have been wrong ; and the opinion that thus bears an anxious reconsideration is more helpful, more sustaining, than one resentfully reaffirmed without hesitation.

This is the gain from doubt. Where you have doubted

carefully, you can have a higher confidence ; and I have no fear that my counsel will unfit you for useful action. You will learn that the majority are often and easily wrong ; and when you have realised how they came to err, when you have rigorously tested your own pre-dilection, you can be firmer and more persistent than they. To many of them, doubt and change of opinion will come from the continuous pressure of unexpected fact ; and if they change brazenly or ignobly, making light of their old obstinacy, they do but reveal their unworthiness. When you have entitled yourselves to condemn them, you will not be more apt than they to shilly-shally. Rather your confidence will outlast theirs ; you will have the satisfaction—a high one as our satis-factions go—of knowing in the end that you have been " in the right with two or three," and that you have not flinched at unpopularity. But when all is said, it is well to remember that high standards of criticism are for ourselves first and last ; that it is more profitable to scan our own slips than to denounce those of other people. Act on Clifford's ethical doctrine by all means and in all serious cases ; but be more concerned to try yourselves by it than to fulminate it against others.

You are much more likely to fall below it than to carry it too far. I would not have you very cautious in every matter of action—in the choosing of your clothes, of a hotel, of a holiday route. Perhaps I am temperamentally given to rapid decision in these minor matters : I fear I have been so in some greater things ; but I reason that in separate or isolated issues it is probably more economical to decide quickly than to weigh lengthily a number of small considerations. And I would not have you unadventurous for yourselves. Where I counsel you to doubt and ponder is in the framing of your beliefs, of your doctrines ; in taking up a political cause, which may mean the helping or hindering of many lives ; in deciding on the rights or wrongs of a war, which is so apt to mean incalculable iniquity and cruelty ; in crediting or discrediting a new teaching, or even a new literary school or method. When you have vigilantly made up your mind, you will act, I trust, energetically. Action is life. A shrewd statesman of two hundred years ago said that " If men would think more they would act less : the greatest part of the business of the world is the effect of not thinking " ; but he had in view the blind activities, the blundering activities. You will find, I hope, that thinking will simply lead you to apply your energies better, and to act in ways that ignorance would not have dreamt of, while abandoning the activities of crude self-assertion in which heady ignorance delights.

If we found that the stupid and ignorant people were always active, and the wiser people usually inactive, we might endorse the old statesman's maxim unreservedly. But I see multitudes of ignorant and bigoted people doing as little as they can help, and many thoughtful and instructed people scheming and acting strenuously. I knew pretty intimately a man famous as an iconoclast, a denier of current dogmas, an " unbeliever " in current sanctities, and his energy of action was to that of most of his gainsayers as the strength of the arm to that of the little finger. And for myself I have always found thinking the best stimulant to action, the best diet for confidence.

Much of what I am saying will be a set of truisms for you when you come to middle age ; but I have little fear that it will be superfluous for you in youth. You will find, I hope, more help to right reasoning in your early environment than I did, and a commoner habit of conscientious thinking than I see around me to-day : if you do not, the world will be no better or happier than it is now. It is not quite inconceivable to me, however, that it may be worse. In any case, you will have your lives to live, and I have reason to believe that you can live them all the better by forming habits of mental circumspection and thoroughness, even if such habits involve a fuller realisation of the lack of them around you. Thought itself is a pleasure, yielding activity, provided it be done by a healthy brain.

On some important matters, such as falling in love and marrying, I shall not attempt to give you advice at all ; because I do not believe that if I did you would act on it. But in the way of thought and action in general, I am fain to hope that I may be able to help you somewhat.

LETTER III

IN the two preceding letters I have urged two counsels
on you : (1) to have no fear of reason, such fear being
its own contradiction ; but to guard against errors of
reasoning by reasoning more thoroughly than before ;
and (2) to be at once slow of belief and slow of disbelief ; disbelief being in effect merely the negative
aspect of the belief that you already know the facts,
or that the facts cannot be as now asserted. But,
unless you are very fortunately organised, you will be
slow to realise how hard it is to act on the second of
those precepts, even when you more thoroughly acquiesce in both. The
difficulty is indeed part of the explanation of that despair
of reason against which the first precept is directed :
we are all so prone to let prejudice shut the door on
judgment, so slow to bring the first-born, bias, under
the control of the second-born, reflection, that when we
sadly scan each other's aberrations the cause of reason
is apt to seem desperate.

Let me, in passing, offer you a consolation. The
element of bias in us is also the element of energy ; and
it is transmutable ; so that when broken to harness, so
to speak, it is as useful a part of character as reason
itself. I speak, you see, in metaphors, for the purpose
of the moment. More scientifically speaking, bias is
simply the first thought ; reason the second thought.
The difficulty is to ensure that the second thought shall
always have its turn.

The older writers in support of religion against " unbelief " used to protest that those who opposed them
were following will rather than reason ; and to a certain
extent they probably spoke truly. Only, the charge
was much more widely and radically true against themselves. All of us tend to argue—that is, when we are
disputing with others—on lines of will. It belongs to

our nature that we should all wish to show good grounds for the belief we now hold, that we should wish to turn out right. But it stands to reason that most men must take more trouble to get out of a belief in which they were brought up than they took to get into it. To have held a belief, and then to have doubted it, is to be potentially a stage farther on the path to right judgment than is one who stays all along where he was put. The latter *may*, after all, be right : but he should clearly be slow to charge on others a following of their carnal inclination. The first carnal inclination is always to think we are right to begin with—that we had not believed in an absurdity. The use-and-wont man may make out a fair case if he can show that the innovator is either adopting a belief which will ostensibly give free scope to his passions, or professing one which may win him worldly advantages ; and it was common to charge the former tendency on " unbelievers," so-called. But as it is historically certain that large bodies of men have claimed a very free scope for their passions on grounds of actual religious belief—belief in the very religion of the use-and-wont man—and as it is tolerably obvious that gain is to be had rather by professing orthodoxy than by opposing it, such arguments are now abandoned by all the more thoughtful of the orthodox. They are valid in their type, but certainly not specially so against minorities. What I am about to say is, so to speak, sauce for both goose and gander ; it bears on all forms and fields of opinion.

We all incur two difficulties in arguing for the opinions we have formed, and against those which clash with them—the difficulty of being candid and the difficulty of being sincere, taking those terms in definitions which give them a moral significance. The two difficulties are at bottom one, and the virtues in question are so likewise. I am wont to say that if we were all perfectly honest we should all be better reasoners, so much bad reasoning being a matter of unreadiness to be fair. In other words, we have so many motives to opinion, so many incitements to *wish* that this or that proposition may be true or untrue, this or that man right or wrong, that we are apt to prejudge as often as to reason. And —such is the paradox of judgment—the play of variety

of motive to belief has often the effect of making us hold
or maintain opinions which contradict each other. If
you will think well of it—so, at least, it has often struck
me—there is something very perplexing and disquieting
in the spectacle of self-contradiction. We nearly all
tend naturally either to assent to any earnest utterance
which does not clash with our previous opinions, or at
least to see in it a " sincere " doctrine which deserves a
respectful attention. But it often happens to us, after
such an assent or appreciation, to find the same teacher
laying down with equal earnestness a contradictory doctrine ; and if we ponder such things deeply they set
up a certain distrust of human nature. As, however,
there is no getting away from human nature, we shall do
well to adjust ourselves to this one of its infirmities as
we do to those of the physical life.

Ueberweg, the eminent German logician, has gravely
and well said that " Absolutely to shun contradiction
is a task demanding so harmonious and thorough a
construction of thought, and at the same time such a
purity and freedom of intention, that to fulfil it remains
an ideal which is ever to be reached proximately only.
Not merely gaps in our investigations, but every kind
of ethical narrow-mindedness, the tenacity of religious,
political, and social prejudices, lead to contradiction."
And again : " Nothing is commoner in difficult problems
than a half and one-sided apprehension of thoughts
strange to us, confounding it with our own opinion,
and then combating this chimæra. The opinion disputed classed under some abstract category or other,
which looks suspicious to common judgment or prejudice,
or else an introduction branding it as heretical, is pre-
fixed to a garbled statement, in order to prevent the
impression which the thought itself even in this form
might make. . . . The contest is transferred to a different province, and, by its construction of suspected
consequences, polemic, which ought to serve for the
common investigation of truth, is degraded to be an
instrument for making attacks on individuals. The experience of all times shows that these perversities are
not solely produced by a specially dull and narrow power
of thought, and by a specially weak and degenerate
will. It is a rare power and structure of thought and

conscience which can keep itself entirely free from them." [1]

And he concludes : " To overcome narrowness, and to enter fully within the circle of an opponent's thoughts and into the motives for his doctrine—which is a very different thing from the languid toleration of indifferentism —presupposes a height of intellectual and ethical character which is not innate either in individuals or in the race of man, but must be acquired by a long and earnest struggle in development. Yet this is the only path which leads man to truth. His judgment only emancipates who has shown himself to be docile."

It is a serious matter, you see ; and I want to impress on you with a little detail the symptoms of the common frailty—or, let us say, the aspects of the paths on which we all tend to go astray.

First, as to candour : the mere constitutional reluctance to admit that we are wrong sets us (1) upon resisting our gainsayer before we weigh his case ; and (2) upon distorting his case when we find it at all difficult to rebut. Further, dislike of a person may incline us (3) to oppose any of his opinions ; or, again, dislike of some of a man's doctrines, after investigation, may move us (4) to negate a new doctrine of his without investigation. Yet again, when we have framed a theory and used it for some time, sheer self-love is apt to make us (5) strain the facts in its favour and give too little weight to the arguments against it. Finally, general sympathy with or antipathy to a cause, or party, or school of opinion, may easily make us prejudge either for or against it on a particular issue. Here we have seven common causes of bad reasoning or unreasoned judgment. Do not then be surprised if you should find what you suspect to be cases in point in these letters ! I am very sure that if I should escape the snares it will be only in virtue of being somewhat anxiously on the look out for them. They are the more insidious because the act of succumbing to them has for us the semblance of loyalty to the right, of service to truth and righteousness. But I think you will agree with me, on reflection, that they all represent lapses from candour.

[1] *System of Logic and History of Logical Doctrines*, Eng. tr. 1871, pp. 248, 527–8.

I define candour, you see, as more than mere avowal of what you see. In that sense, a deeply prejudiced person is candid in respect that his prejudice really prevents his properly seeing the other side. So to define the word is to make it insignificant, or at least practically useless, as it will then mean only " not fraudulent or malicious." All considerate usage makes it suggest the taking of some trouble to be fair, the attainment of a somewhat difficult attitude, or else a great natural gift for fairness. It is common, however, when a prejudiced person is charged with being uncandid, to hear it said for him that he is " sincere." Now, I propose that we should so define sincerity as to make it, like candour, mean more than mere abstinence from calculated wrongdoing. In the loose sense I allude to, any man who is in a passion is sincere ; and any unfair or inconsistent person may be so. I can see no use in the word if it is not to be more stringently defined.

According to some etymologists, the Latin word *sincerus*, from which ours comes, originally meant *sine cera*, " without wax," and was applied to statues to signify that they were not, as often happened, flawed or broken in the stone and puttied-up with wax to pass muster. That has always seemed to me a funny and questionable etymology ; and I see that some scholars surmise the original form of the term to have meant " having (or consisting of) one wax," which is at first sight not much more satisfying. But either etymology, even if wrong, may serve to suggest the proper and useful force of the term. Sincerity, to be a deeply significant term, should mean not merely the state of believing what you say at any one moment—a state normal to many foolish or thoughtless or malevolent people—but the state of attained or perfected consistency.

Let me illustrate my meaning. Suppose that a certain political leader, rightly resenting a breach of law among the party opposed to him, insists that the act ought to be severely punished ; and that nevertheless, when an exactly similar act is committed among his own party, he makes light of the offence and finds excuses for it, then he is clearly " inconsistent." We so describe his conduct in its intellectual or logical aspect. I argue that, in its moral aspect, we should call him insincere.

It matters not, I say, whether at the moment of self-stultification he did or did not remember how he had formerly denounced the kind of conduct he now palliates.

If indeed he remembered his former verdict, repented of it, and avowed his repentance, he would be neither insincere nor inconsistent; he would simply be changing his opinion and avowing so. Inconsistency means not change of principle, but failure to conform to the principle you still profess to hold. Consistency is not the same thing as constancy. But if you profess to act on a given principle, yet under the sway of partisan or other interest either forget it or set it aside, you are not merely, I say, inconsistent, you are insincere. You do not thoroughly and deeply hold the principle you profess; it is not a part of your habitual code; it is a pretext you adopt at convenience, or merely to gratify a particular aversion. Some forms of inconsistency are indeed so insignificant on the moral side that it would be doing a violence to our term to say they proved insincerity; but where inconsistency of conduct *plus* doctrine amounts to committing serious unfairness, the deflection from intellectual consistency is rightly to be stigmatised on the moral side as insincerity. If not—if sincerity be compatible with meting out different measures to men and causes in terms of your mood or your partiality—what is sincerity worth? We *mean* the term to be complimentary: is it really so when so laxly used?

It may be argued against me, I can see, that insofar as I make the terms inconsistency and insincerity mean the same thing I am reducing the utility of one of them; but I would answer that I am making them apply to different aspects of the thing—the intellectual or logical, and the moral. I am seeking, in short, to introduce at *this* point a moral element into the characterisation of error. This raises the old question whether " error " is ever to be regarded as " guilty." Either (it may be said) a man knows that he is perverting the truth, in which case he is not erring but lying, or he does not know, in which case he is to be compassionated, not condemned.

I answer that the problem is nearly on a par with that raised in the expression " culpable negligence."

We all admit that we may be " culpably careless " ; in other words, we agree that it is desirable to keep current the opinion that a carelessness which endangers life or limb is seriously " wrong." (Whether it ought to be " punished " as it sometimes is in the case of an engine-driver or pointsman is another matter : I am strongly inclined to think such " punishments " even more uselessly cruel than others.) It seems clear that social stigma has an educative effect as applied to injurious negligence no less than to injurious aggression. Now, if carelessly inconsistent reasoning and conduct—inconsistency of one with the other, or of parts of either with other parts—involves demonstrably unjust criticism, to say nothing of far more extensive and grievous evil (as in the promotion of an unjust war), the application of the term insincerity to the moral aspect of such inconsistency is as well warranted as the expression " culpable negligence " usually is.

Broadly speaking, we all tend to be more or less inconsistent, and we all tend to be more or less insincere. Let us, however, make the term a test for our own thinking, as I am seeking to do now, before we use it to impeach others ; even as we do well to apply Clifford's stringent law against undue belief more readily to our own thought than to that of others. If I find that, seeking to carry a certain point, I once advanced a certain proposition in one connection ; and that, forgetting this, but not proceeding on any new knowledge, I advanced at another time a contrary proposition in another connection to carry another point, I ought to admit that I have been insincere, and it is my duty to recant one of my propositions if recantation be feasible. I had presumably been arguing from hand to mouth, saying one thing or another without thorough or weighed conviction, playing fast and loose with truth and demonstration.

You will now see better what I mean when I say it is hard to be candid and sincere in argument. On a multitude of issues we frame propositions as we go along, on the most various motives. Mere objection to being strongly importuned by a new doctrine may tempt us to use against it an argument which, when faithfully applied, counters some other opinion of our own, and is therefore either fallacious or a demonstration that we hold by a fallacy. At one point or other, then, we have been insincere. Someone, again, utters a dictum which disparages one of our heroes or makes light of one of our theories or conclusions, and in our resentment we so describe the annoying proposition as to make it appear other than it is. When we so act we deserve severe terms at the hands of any moralist who is himself more scrupulous. We have been uncandid. To discover afterwards that we have in this fashion penned an injustice or a misrepresentation should be to any one of us a painful and humbling experience. Yet there is a shamelessness about such things on the part of many that seems to me almost more odious than shamelessness about acts of fraud ; and it is because I would fain think of you as incapable of it that I thus repeatedly press upon you the moral aspects of bad reasoning.

Intellectual honesty, I am satisfied, is much rarer than pecuniary honesty, probably because the stress of social evolution has run so much more to regulating the physical and commercial than the intellectual relations of men. No doubt it follows that intellectual deformity analogous to kleptomania is relatively frequent—that many men really cannot see straight in discussion, even when they are used to it. But new perception of risks is for each of us a new element of " determination " ; and if you realise that I am urging these things on you seriously for your good I may be saving you from some slips.

I would ask you to take note, then, (1) that malice is very apt to make us positively misread an opponent's meaning. Of this I have had some amusing experiences in reviews of my own books. In one, for instance, I chanced to speak of a certain book as published in " 1790, and later." The type was large and clear ; but one hostile critic actually cited the words as " 1790, or later," and pointed to them as proof that I had an absurdly happy-go-lucky way of guessing at the date of a book when I might ascertain it by enquiry. The fact was that the book had been published in 1790, and expanded in a later edition, hence the manner of my reference. Now, that critic cannot have been wilfully lying ; the perversion was too imbecile, too exposable, to be deliberately made. But, as his review showed, he was very angry, and his malice positively affected his vision. Less gross cases are frequent in reviewing.

Even without malice, however, one is very apt (2) to misstate an argument one does not like. I have seen this done many a time by men not hasty or passionate in temper, and much disposed to lay stress on the importance of ethics. They simply lacked precision of perception on the side of dialectics, and had never realised the need for moral discipline in such matters. A proposition that jarred on their feelings spontaneously took for them a more repulsive form ; like some nervous artists, they instinctively exaggerated the feature they did not like, seeing it through a medium of disturbed æsthesis. Such a tendency must be hard to guard against ; and if either of you should chance to be organised in that way my present preaching may avail you little. Still, I will lay down a few prescriptions, some of which might be useful.

1. In such matters we ought to ask ourselves, as it were by rule, whether we are doing as we would be done by.

2. Even if we are, so to speak, in a " state of war " with any writer or disputant, and feel that he ought to be discredited, a patient analysis of his argument is the best preparation for an effective reply. If he is quite wrong, we shall realise this more fully and clearly after repeated reflection ; if he is not quite wrong, we are much likelier when patient to guard against indiscriminate or blundering denial of what he says. The clearest perception, as a rule, will always yield the tersest and most clear-cut rebuttal.

In other words, conscientiousness is a great help to right reasoning. Perhaps, as I have said, most of the bad argument in the world is the result of sheer unreadiness to give full weight to an opposing argument.

3. Make it a point, if possible, to argue against yourself before you undertake to maintain any position. That is, try to conceive at every step how an opponent might answer you. I say " if possible," as I am not sure to what extent this habit may be acquirable or may be a special idiosyncrasy. In any case, I can assure you that it is well worth your while to try to

form it. It has sometimes happened to me to convert myself completely from a particular view by checking it when I set about propounding it.

But with all this, remember, it is of supreme and constant importance to *know* the subject under discussion. Some logicians, including Kant, have sought to keep logic as it were independent of things, insisting that it has to deal with laws of thought which stand in their own right. They mean that the principles on which we draw a logical conclusion are the same for all men and in all cases, and that by them we can judge whether a given argument is sound even if it be on a subject we have not studied—or rather, that every student, no matter what his subject, must, if he would reason soundly, come to those principles, which we find on reflection in our own minds. But even as regards the universal principles, it is certain that only after long use of the judging faculty on things, on the problems of daily life, did men attain to the power of stating those principles, and holding at all steadily by them in a complicated argument. And since, as I have said, many if not most errors result from imperfect or false information, or prejudice, rather than from wrong processes of reasoning on facts, it follows that improvement depends very much on further search for facts.

It is not merely that study will inform you of the error of a given premiss, as in the case of that statement about the religion of Teutons and Celts; but that it will help you in a general way to a judgment on probabilities. Having detected one general error, you will be on your guard against similar errors; and having reached some general truths about, say, the processes of human affairs or natural phenomena, you will be helped (though here you must be on your guard against new error) to look for sequences in a new set of facts. Above all, the more you know the better are you fitted to give provisional assent to or dissent from a new proposition.

Take for instance the problem of the historic actuality of the Gospel Jesus. To any one brought up as a believing Christian, and even to most people brought up in or converted to what we call rationalism or naturalism, the suggestion that " no such person as *that* Jesus " ever existed is apt to seem merely preposterous. It seemed so to me when I heard it at the age of twenty or more. It is not that even when we set aside all the miracles there is anything very lifelike in the narrative that is left. An average novel is much more lifelike ; but as to the novel we assume from the start that it is a fiction, whereas we had all assumed from the start that the gospels told, with whatever fabulous addenda, of the life of a real personage ; and the first shock of a challenge to that view is too disturbing to permit of a prompt seizure of the essentials of the problem.

It is precisely the least prepared believer who is most confident. When the student proceeds to weigh the arguments he becomes gradually less surprised at the challenge, even though he adheres to his first belief. He is forced to acknowledge that a narrative which abounds in myths of action—stories of unbelievable events—is open to suspicion in its narratives of mere teaching, or narratives of events which, like those in novels, *might* really have happened. When he clearly realises that the gospels are a patchwork, frequently eked out and interpolated, he admits that it is difficult to settle what parts are primordial, and to what extent those parts are trustworthy. When further he learns that even some parts supposed to be primordial, such as the Sermon on the Mount, are really compilations from earlier and contemporary Jewish literature, he cannot but concede that his right to his old certainty is much shaken. And when, finally, he faces the problem as to the apparently complete ignorance of the Jesuine teaching on the part of the author or authors of the Pauline epistles, which are ostensibly the earliest documents, he must, if he be candid, grant that there are clear and fair reasons for questioning the historic actuality of the Gospel Jesus. He may for various reasons continue to believe in and affirm it, but he will neither put aside the doubt with the confident contempt of the ignorant man nor think to settle the question once for all by mere *a priori* argument such as the claim that the story *cannot* be an aggregation of fictions, or that " there *must* have been a real founder." Neither will he say, as an unprepared person is apt to say offhand, that " if we believe in the existence of Julius Cæsar we must believe in the existence of Jesus Christ; we have the same kinds of evidence in the two cases." He will have realised, after working at the problem, that the two cases are profoundly different; and that just as we may reasonably be sure of the historic actuality of Charlemagne and reject as a fable the story of William Tell, though the latter is the later, so we may be sure of the actuality of Socrates and at least doubt the actuality of the Gospel Jesus.

A priori or abstract reasoning, in fine, can settle only abstract problems: all problems of concrete existence and occurrence are conditioned by testimony, and they are to be solved only after careful reasoning on the nature and value of the testimony concerned. Remember that just as people now scoff at doubts of the actuality of Jesus, they scoffed not very long ago at doubts of the historic actuality of Adam and Eve and the siege of Troy; and, a little earlier, at doubts concerning King Arthur and the miracles of the saints. Our opinions are constantly liable to be coloured or determined by our presuppositions in general; and just as men in the Middle Ages had no difficulty in crediting stories which we see to be absurd, because their education began with such stories, so even an able man who to-day is educated in a religious creed will be a bad reasoner on that creed unless he takes patient pains to test it. There have been many cases of acute men of science—such as Faraday, Kelvin, and Croll—who applied their minds with originality and success to problems of natural science, and remained astonishingly credulous and uncritical on questions of religious history and dogma. To the study of the latter they had no strong natural bent; and as they failed to make up for lack of bent by special study, they remained ignorant thinkers on one set of subjects, while they were experts in others. When you come to understand how given men are thus variously gifted and deficient, educated and uneducated, you will be saved, perhaps, from a good deal of perplexity and discouragement.

Let me give you an interesting illustration. The late Dr. James Croll, who began life with little schooling and no money-advantages, gradually qualified himself, despite many breakdowns and hindrances of health, to deal

authoritatively with such problems as those of glacial
action, ocean currents, and planetary history. I am
not entitled to a definite personal opinion on the value
of his results in these matters, but I find it highly
rated by competent men of science. On the other hand
I find him to have retained in religion an attitude so
unintelligent that I should have pronounced it foolish
if I had not, from a study of his life, learned to see
in it the result primarily of education and secondarily
of the sheer curtailment of his mental life by pain and
disease, and the absorption of what brain energy he
had in other problems. In his latter years he could
use his brain thoroughly for only an hour or two at a
time ; and it is impossible to read his autobiographic
sketch without warm sympathy and admiration for the
patient courage with which he bore up under a series
of desperate infirmities, doing what he could to the end.
Some of his moral qualities were of the rarest kind.

By nature the man was an acute, candid, and scrupulous reasoner ; and while his bent was to physical science
he greatly preferred those sciences in which ratiocination
counted for most, and the mastery and enumeration
of details least. Thus he " positively shrank " from
chemistry and geology, though he was led to pay heed
to the latter science partly by way of money-earning
avocation and partly by the need for facts in connection
with his speculations on cosmic time. Such, too, was
his thoroughness that while engaged in his early man-
hood as a tea-dealer he gave all his spare time for at
least a year and a half to mastering the debate on
Freewill, as brought before him by the treatise of that
very remarkable thinker Jonathan Edwards—who, by
the way, was one of the ancestors of your mother.
More than five times did Croll read the book, always
unable to find a flaw in the reasoning, yet long unable
to agree to its conclusions. Only when the strength
of the argument was finally established for him by
the failure of all attempts to refute it did he submit.
Now, this tells of an uncommonly honest and sure
though slow mind. Only men with good reasoning
powers are thus impressed by Jonathan Edwards. Yet
Croll, while reasoning thus deeply and logically on one
aspect of theology, never proceeded to sift the quasi-

historical premisses on which Edwards as a Christian proceeded, and remained to the end of his life satisfied with his earlier creed that " salvation was entirely of free grace." As he says :

> Simple trust in Christ's vicarious death gave me complete peace of mind and true happiness, a peace which the world can neither give nor take away. The agnostic will smile at my experience. How different would he feel if he experienced this blessed peace himself.
>
> > The love of Jesus, what it is
> > None but his loved ones know.[1]

Here we have the complete renunciation of the procedure by which Croll attained his scientific results and even his acquiescence in the argument of Edwards. He wilfully assumes that " the agnostic " can never have such peace of mind as his—a childish delusion. He has never asked whether his special satisfaction is not exactly like that of religionists of other creeds, including men in the savage state of culture, whose way of holding and acting on the belief in an atoning sacrifice would have been to him morally horrible, though philosophically on the same plane of belief as his. Now, had Croll been able to give his attention and thought to history and anthropology as he gave them to matters of natural science ; had he begun his serious religious reading by a study of the article on " Atonement " in the old *Penny Cyclopædia*, and carried it on through Tylor and Darwin and Robertson Smith and Clifford, Strauss and Baur and Renan and Havet, he would, I think, have become incapable of his early belief in " salvation by atonement." He would have transcended it as men transcend the ideals of their childhood. The whole problem would have assumed for him a different aspect ; and what was latterly for him an emotional need would have become as remote from him as the inebriate's craving for alcohol or the invalid's for morphia. He would have seen, too, without difficulty, that the close and acute argumentation of Jonathan Edwards on Freewill has no valid connection whatever with the dogmas of Christianity, which in fact serve to degrade his philosophic work into a miserable ministry to superstition.

[1] *Autobiographical Sketch of James Croll*, 1896, pp. 17–23.

The moral is that our knowledge makes a matrix, a " climate," in which our reasonings are well or ill nourished, developed or stunted. Not all men, indeed, suffer as Croll did from the lack of relevant culture. Men far inferior to him in power of speculation on physical problems, and even in power of connected ratiocination, might have a natural power of judgment which with no special culture would withhold or withdraw them from his more grotesque religious beliefs. As I have elsewhere claimed to show, there are in all stages of civilisation some men naturally averse to the current absurdities of religious creed, varying towards good sense as others vary towards other forms of faculty. But for the average run of us special culture makes nearly all the difference between acquiescence in and release from common delusions.

All that I have said, then, as to the need for slowness alike of belief and of disbelief points not to a disregard for testimony and lore, but to a zealous gathering of it. For though a little-read man with good judgment is preferable to a widely read man with none, it remains true that knowledge is the soil in which judgment waxes, and that every process of reasoning tends to be deepened and refined as it is based on a widened knowledge of the sum of things. " With all thy getting, get understanding," said the wisdom-loving Hebrew. I am trying to help you on that course ; but you will best help yourselves, perhaps, by taking pains to know the facts on any issue on which you seek to form a judgment.

LETTER IV

You will remember that, in speaking of the theories of
Dr. Croll, I said I had no right to a definite opinion
on their value. It probably occurred to you in reading
that some such avowal has often to be made by sensible
people, and that it is not always easy to decide where
it is rightly called for. I have been arguing, in effect,
that it ought often to be made where it is not, as when
people pronounce without any special study on such a
problem as the historic actuality of the Gospel Jesus.
But after we have recognised the unwisdom of such
pronouncements, it is a serious matter for every one
of us to decide how far he shall be content either to
remain neutral on current questions or to rely on the
judgment of specialists. One of the standing perplexities
of life is this of " the influence of authority in matters of
opinion " ; and you are likely to be met by claims
on the subject which will give you trouble. This is
another aspect of the discipline of opinion, above considered.

It is clear that we cannot investigate all subjects
for ourselves, or even all the details of every subject
of which we make a special study. In biology, for instance, even the biologist takes the observations of many
investigators for granted, provided that they seem to
him competently done, and in no way inconsistent with
his previous knowledge. The non-specialist, again, must
either keep his mind pretty much a blank on many
great branches of science or accept as trustworthy the
results set forth by men who seem to him to know
their business and to think clearly. For such cases it
is a sufficient common-sense rule to regard as provision-
ally true or probable the teachings which pass current as
authoritative among scientific specialists, simply taking
care to remember that here we " walk by faith," and

never joining in any resistance to any other teaching without taking great pains to understand the merits of the dispute. If we do not take such trouble we act unworthily and blameably in lending our voices to cry down any innovator.

It is to be observed, however, that many people, without making any independent investigation whatever, will give the most emphatic endorsement to some scientific or other propositions, and treat with angry contempt those who do not accept them. It is the curse of " faith " commonly so called that it has inspired multitudes during many centuries thus to be most zealous precisely where they have thought least for themselves. But the tendency is not confined to the field of religion. The food-value of many substances commonly eaten, for instance, is very variously estimated ; and some of us persist in eating some things (such as ordinary bread) which are often declared to be innutritious in comparison with others equally available. We do this either because we doubt the alleged innutritiousness, not finding proof of it in our own experience, or because we dislike the foods urged on us in preference. In this, many of us are no doubt regrettably careless. But on the other hand we have cause to distrust the judgment of many who, having no skill or practice whatever in chemical or physiological analysis, not only adopt a precise doctrine of food values, but deride those who do not do likewise. Such persons exhibit the primary bias to easy belief and disbelief, in the form of a complete submission to a given authority, which they seek to impose on others in a spirit of fanaticism. Even if they happen to be right, they are so " by chance," in a dangerously uncritical way. Of course a man who carefully observes the effects of given foods on himself is well entitled to urge his conclusions on others. But even he need remember that it is hazardous to make a general induction of the kind from one or a few cases. Given foods would seem to suit different persons in very different degrees.

So far the course is pretty clear. Where " authority " clearly turns upon special knowledge, in a field which we have not the time to explore for ourselves, we all accept authority as a working principle. I take from experts the latest theory of the chemical structure of sugar, as I take from an explorer his account of a country that I do not expect to visit. They may err : therefore I must not be their partisan against those who appear competently to criticise them ; but under that reservation I take the risk of being misled. In the case of Dr. Croll's theory of ocean currents I remain neutral, because it does not rest upon any specialist knowledge that I lack, and fails to convince me, yet without leaving me at all sure that it is wrong. To come to a more definite opinion would cost me more time and study than I can give to the matter. In such a case, one may be content to be neutral. But there are certain provinces of opinion in which it behoves us all to think and *decide* for ourselves if we would be valid personalities, or fulfil worthily our duties as citizens. To take on authority our notions of right and wrong, of what is just or expedient in politics, of what is true in religion or religious history, would be to become contemptible, or at least intellectually null.

To the greater part of this last proposition most men will assent ; though I have latterly seen educated men, including at least one of professorial status, avow that they form their opinion on the justice of an act of international aggression by simple acceptance of the views of one alleged " expert." But while few will justify this course, which means a renunciation of a main part of the duties of a citizen in such a State as ours, there are many who, going with my claim so far, will draw the line at religion, and argue that there we ought to bow to authority. Let us see what this position involves.

The first and simplest argument of a religious person as against one who rejects his beliefs, or one who gives them different dogmatic form, is (a) that man must bow to a revelation from " God," or (b) that in religious matters the proper safeguard against the fallibility of individual opinion is the authority of the head of the historic Church. The rational answer to the first assertion is that it assumes the very point in dispute : that most religions have claimed to be supernatural revelations ; that it must lie with each one of us to decide for himself whether any is ; and that the man who alleges

" revelation " is finally doing so on the strength of his
personal opinion. To the second formula the answer
is, again, that we actually use our private judgment
when we reason that the Church or its head is the
proper authority on religious truth. Either we are re-
peating a mere rote lesson, or we are passing an individual judgment. The man who puts his opinions for
shaping in the hands of a given authority is either not
reasoning at all, or is proceeding on his own judgment
exactly as when he chooses a doctor. And it turns out
in practice that among Roman Catholics, who nominally
stand for the principle of authority in religion, the
argument finally takes the form that, just as some
men have a special genius for medicine or war, so some
have a special genius for religious truth, and that this
genius is found collectively among religious people and
supremely in the organised Church, which embodies both
the special gift and the maximum of educative experience. Such at least seems to be the argument of the
late Cardinal Newman, in his *Grammar of Assent* [1] and
elsewhere.

But here again there is either an appeal to reason or
there is not ; and in the end Cardinal Newman does
not rest on his mere argument that we should recognise
the gift of religious people for religion, but actually
appeals to us, on the most hackneyed lines of Protestant
argument, to accept the Christian religion as something
visibly supernatural in the manner of its propagation and
acceptance. He had previously argued that in all fields
there are special gifts of perception ; and he had protested against Paley's undertaking to prove the truth of
Christianity to anybody on common-sense lines, warmly
disparaging " the conduct of those who resolve to treat
the Almighty with dispassionateness, a judicial temper,
clear-headedness, and candour." Here, as usual, he has
" begged the question " ; he is angry with those who
need to be converted to his creed. And yet in the end,
tacitly admitting the futility of such language, which
appeals only to those who need not be appealed to,
he falls back on the usual orthodox methods of re-
futing Gibbon's thesis that Christianity arose in a natural,
sequent, and intelligible fashion.

[1] Ch. ix, " The Illative Sense."

This, I think, is the invariable outcome of Roman Catholic reasoning in the hands of the ablest Catholics. Newman indeed does not strike me as at all a coherent reasoner in comparison with some others of his Church ; but in point of the power of seeing by flashes deep into a problem he is entitled to be ranked high. To follow his *Grammar of Assent* closely is to realise that on any line of reasoning he soon reached the knowledge that he believed because he wanted to. For this course he seeks to find a sanction alternately in the ordinary procedure of human nature—as if the bald fact that men commonly reach their beliefs in a certain way were a justification of them—and in the suggestion that some men's thought on a given theme has a superiority against which there is no use in arguing. Apparently, however, he always realises at this stage that on that view every creed and every iconoclast is free to make the same claim, and the argument for authority dies away in a bad demonstration.

There remains a possible difficulty on one score : namely, that many persons avowedly believe on " authority " certain propositions which they do not understand. Those propositions come to them, they say, from sources which they have found to be otherwise trustworthy ; from a Church and a scripture and a set of teachers whom they find to be profoundly wise where they can check them by reason ; and when such a consensus of authority lays down a mystical doctrine, unintelligible to ordinary judgment, it is to be accepted (so runs the argument) as a divine mystery. Over this question you may be met by the kind of argument contained in the familiar story about the college dignitary who, when a young man said in his presence, " I believe nothing that I cannot understand," answered, " Then you will have the shortest creed of any man I know." In that argument, as commonly used, there is a bad verbal confusion. People who use it do not seem to me to have settled what they mean by " what I understand."

In all likelihood (taking the story to be true) the young man meant, " I do not believe propositions which I cannot understand " ; and if that was his meaning he was speaking reasonably. The academic dignitary, on the other hand, seems to have understood him to mean, " I do not believe in the occurrence of processes whose nature I do not understand." So to interpret him was not very candid or sensible ; we may suppose that the dignitary was provoked by an air of bumptiousness in his utterance, and resentfully wanted to snub him. If, however, the dignitary really resented and condemned the avowal " I do not believe *propositions* which I cannot understand," his resentment was that of an " irrational " person, as the phrase goes. And as many of the religious people of whom I have spoken do notoriously profess to believe propositions they do not understand, we shall do well to examine their position.

It is clear, to begin with, that we must often give our assent to statements of the occurrence of processes whose *nature* we do not understand. Take for instance the law of gravitation. It would be straining the use of the word to say that we " understand " the universal process or phenomenon of gravity ; though we may rightly say we understand given phenomena in terms of the law of gravitation, which we take for granted. To explain gravity itself, many hypotheses have been and are being made, in terms of molecular motion ; and it may be that one day we shall " understand " gravitation in terms of some one or more of those hypotheses. Meantime, we assent to the proposition which formulates for us the subsistence of gravitation ; and we do this because we *understand the proposition* and recognise the evidence in support of it. So with many other matters. We can understand propositions which affirm the normal occurrence of " mysterious " processes—that is, processes which we cannot yet analyse in terms of other processes—and when we are satisfied with the evidence we say we believe those propositions.

It is quite another matter, however, to say we can or should assent to *propositions* which we do not understand. So far was the young man of the story from being wrong in repudiating belief in such propositions, he might, I should say, have ventured to assert that *no* man believes in propositions which he does not understand. How can there be " belief " on such lines ? If I say " Abracadabra sings green," it matters not whether any one professes assent ; there is no belief, simply because there is nothing understood. And if such a phrase be offered to me as a divine truth by men who find it in a " sacred " book and say they are ecstatically sure of its divinity, it is all the same. Belief is assent to an understood proposition, whether or not formally expressed. Try, if you like, to think of yourself as believing that greenness cures toothache, and that pleasure makes boots !

Let us apply this test to a religious doctrine over which men frequently profess to give a devout assent without understanding it. The Christian creed affirms that Deity consists of three " persons " which are perfectly distinct yet perfectly one ; not three Gods, but one God ; yet not one person but three ; one being Father, the second Son, and the third Holy Spirit. Now, it is quite possible so to paraphrase the bare formula " Trinity in Unity " as to make it intelligible : you have only to say that " person " means in the strict Latin sense *persona*, a character or function, and that one Deity is " three persons " in the sense that he " plays three parts " or has " three character aspects." But such a rationalisation is not orthodox Christian doctrine ; every intelligible compromise of the kind has been branded as antitrinitarian heresy ; and the Trinitarian creeds continue to insist on the personality of the three " persons " in the normal sense of the term. The creed is in fact avowedly an affirmation of the unintelligible : the Christian is called upon to accept it as an incomprehensible proposition ; and the orthodox Christian does so accept it, avowing that he " believes " the doctrine as being given by supernatural revelation. The more thoughtful believers, on challenge, will say that they are satisfied on reasonable grounds (1) of the supreme wisdom of the Scriptures in general, (2) of the spiritual genius of multitudes of the men and women who have accepted the dogma ; or, if they be Roman Catholics, they may put it (3) that they are by historical study satisfied of the fulfilment of the Gospel promise of divine-indwelling to " the Church " ; and that on that score they believe what the Church officially teaches.

You will readily see, I think, the rational answer to such avowals. In the first place, the assent given to the dogma is merely nominal : it is not belief ; it is a make-believe. The proposition that three literal persons are literally one—that three separate Almighties are but one Almighty—is believed by nobody, let him say what he will. The "believing" Christian is either playing the part of a parrot or is spending his life in alternation between the two "heresies" of Tritheism and Sabellianism. And the final solution of this strange dispute is to be found in realising *why* men came to set up such an astonishing shibboleth, and to maintain it. Broadly speaking, it was in this wise. Long before Christianity, priesthoods found their advantage in grouping as husband and wife and child, or in some other relation, deities who had been separately worshipped ; or in distinguishing among a multitude of deities sets who had long been reputed to be so related. The beginnings of the idea probably lie in the remotest ages of human culture, when Gods and Goddesses of Sun and Earth, River and Field, were figured in terms of human personalities and relationships. As a result of all that primeval guesswork, Triads were common in the Babylonian and Egyptian world before our era.

In the earliest Christian documents the Triad idea is not present ; it arose, like most of the rites of the cult, by way of assimilation of convenient doctrines from other systems ; men trained in Egyptian and Syrian mysticisms turning the formulas of these to the uses of the new system. We need not here ask whether they were "dishonest" or merely "confused." In our strict sense of the term they were both ; they could not be "sincere" because their intellectual processes were so undisciplined, so lax, so incompetent. Once set up, however, the Trinitarian formula became a stumbling-block for the more intelligent theologians ; and many of these sought to rationalise it in some such fashion as I have above indicated. But to do his was to put in jeopardy one or other of the elements of the faith on which its prestige appeared to rest. If "the Son" were defined as a mere "phase" of the Deity, the gospel story in general and the doctrines of the divine sacrifice and the eucharist were resolved into mere avowed metaphors ; the hold of the priesthood on the hopes and fears of the multitude would be gone ; and with the faith would vanish the revenue. If, on the other hand, the separateness of "the Son" from the Father were alone insisted on, the monotheistic basis, emphasised in the Old Testament, would be upset, and Christianity would be only one school of polytheism competing with others. The insoluble dilemma was met by an unintelligible formula ; the Church affirmed both sides of a contradiction ; the religious habit sufficed to make the little-reasoning majority acquiesce ; and there the dogma stands to-day, a shibboleth fit for savages, the intellectual scandal and demoralisation of the Christian system.

I have gone thus briefly into a historic matter in order to bring home to you on another line the truth of the proposition that men's errors and absurdities are the results more often of overruling motives of interest and prejudice than of simple fallacy committed in good faith. To guess wrong is human, so to speak ; to fix a wrong guess in an inconceivable dogma is sacerdotal. But sacerdotalism is merely the organisation of error on the lines of a particular set of interests : other interests pervert us in other ways.

It is hardly necessary to point out, further, the fallacy involved in saying : " I find the Scriptures in general marvellously wise ; the Scriptures lay down the doctrine of the Trinity, therefore I accept it ; the Church, too, is collectively wise above any individual, I therefore accept the Church's interpretation." It might suffice to answer (1) that " the Scriptures " are demonstrably the work of many hands ; but (2) even if they were not, the general wisdom of a scripture would be no reason why we should go through the form of accepting from it a proposition to which we can attach no meaning. In point of fact, however, almost no man now believes every *intelligible* statement made in the Christian scriptures ; there is therefore a plain " insincerity " in the official maintenance of an unintelligible proposition on scriptural grounds. Many believers, I have noticed, are ready to reduce to allegory or trope plain Biblical teachings which happen to be inconvenient, yet persist in giving a literal force to dogmas that convey no idea whatever. Such are the fruits of the principle of " authority."

Is there then any reasonable ground for admitting " authority " in matters of religion ? The answer is, I think, that insofar as our opinions in this field turn upon special knowledge, such as that of experts in Hebrew and Assyriology, we have to depend on their research, remembering always that one expert may contradict another ; but that as regards the great problems of belief in a definable deity and a " moral government of the universe," as well as with regard to the moral soundness of religious precepts and dogmas, we must either think matters out for ourselves or confessedly remain on the intellectual plane of Catholic peasants. The man who tells me that I am spiritually blind, and that he or another has spiritual vision, merely invites me to tell him that he is given over to a strong delusion, and that what he calls special insight is in my opinion special blindness—an inability to reason intelligently from the facts which lie before us all.

Certainly there are great differences in men's faculty for philosophic thought and for moral judgment : we all make such discriminations among those we know and among the writers we read. And when we find ourselves indisposed to agree on a point of philosophy or ethics with one whom we have usually felt to be highly competent, we naturally hesitate long before deciding. If on a question of moral theory or practice I find myself diverging from Spinoza, or Fichte, or Sidgwick, or Spencer—much more if I am diverging from all four—I shall think twice, or thrice, or twenty times before I make up my mind. But in all such cases, observe, we are finally relying on our own judgment, even if we see fit to yield to the " authority " ; and, whereas we do that to the extent of taking a risk when we choose to follow one physician's rule rather than another's, we there do the best we can for ourselves, we not being physicians ; while to " take a risk " by way of accepting a moral principle, or a philosophic principle which has moral consequences, merely because we think highly of the man who lays it down, is not to do the best we can for ourselves, but to surrender our moral dignity and prepare the atrophy of our moral sense.

It is not enough to remember this for ourselves : we should constantly remember it for others. A thoughtful and well-informed man may naturally be impatient of the " self-opinionated " opposition of the ill-informed ;

but if he be morally as well as technically wise he will always remember that there is no moral or educational value in the mere assent of an ill-informed person on a matter of general judgment, as distinguished from one of special knowledge ; and that it is better for the less wise man to think wrongly for himself than to be right by the mere chance of his obedience to a teacher who may happen to be right. One is sometimes tempted to think that a great many people could not do better than follow unquestioningly the guidance of someone wiser than themselves. But rightly to choose a guide, to begin with, is a matter that would call for careful judgment ; and if the chooser should first make a wise choice and afterwards be in the position of following the guide when the guide is wrong, he will in the terms of the case have lost some of his power of judging —that is to say, he will have sunk to a lower moral and intellectual level.

Let us, then, never seek a mere docile assent, even from the unwise. They ought, indeed, like the wise, to practise a candid and careful attention ; we may rightly ask them for that if we in turn accord it ; but we should not better them or ourselves if we could induce them to accept opinions on " authority." The authority who persuades them to do so is in a fair way to acquire all the vices of the historic priest. Being accustomed to deference, he is easily enraged by contradiction, and thus himself loses the precious power of learning new truth. He then figures as a possessor of power without the qualifications for its safe use. Better that the unwise should err in opinion than that they should be occasionally and unwittingly right on the authority of one thus sure to be at times seriously wrong. The only way by which they can be made really wiser is that of thinking for themselves, tentatively following indeed what guidance appeals to them, but never without weighing for themselves the opinion in hand, if it be not one that only expert knowledge can test.

Perhaps this strain of thought may strike you as platitudinous. If so, so much the better—so much the better, that is, if you have already seen the point for yourselves. It was powerfully put long ago, on somewhat different lines, by John Stuart Mill in his essay

On Liberty ; and, in another aspect, it was put less vividly but still well a generation before him, by Samuel Bailey in his *Essays on the Formation and Publication of Opinions*. But I feel sure that the matter needs to be brought home afresh to each new generation : the perception of such truth is not inherited.

To conclude : You will sometimes find yourselves in the position of having formed an opinion which some one with greater authority—that is, ostensibly fuller knowledge of the subject—contravenes. If you are quite sure of his fuller knowledge, you will at once, I hope, suspend your judgment till you have studied the matter further. If, after all the study you can give it, you are still at a loss to acquiesce, you will best preserve your integrity and your power of future judgment by either reserving the question as doubtful or clearly working out your reasons for rejecting the " authoritative " opinion. If the matter be one of what we call " taste," that is, a question of judgment on the æsthetic merit of a picture, or a poem, or a novel, or a piece of music, the proper course remains the same. If you cannot really admire a picture or composition that is highly praised by people accustomed to judge of such things, you will never, I trust, proceed to affect to do so. You will be content, I hope, to admit your difficulty and await the probable effect of further experience on your taste. To admire to order, to admire in advance the things praised by eminent critics, is not very good for any of us. We are all, I fear, rather apt to do it in youth ; but even then we instinctively object to it when we see it done by others, feeling that such foregone or fashion-following opinion is a sign of either weakness or immaturity of character.

But in saying all this I do not forget or cancel my warnings to you against letting self-will keep you wrong. We all develop in taste, as in thought, up to a certain point at least ; and you must have matured much faster than I did if you are not often startled on a return to a book or a picture that you spontaneously admired a few years ago. Such experience ought to be educative. Some people, I think, flaunt their changes rather gratuitously, making one feel that they admire lightly and lightly alter ; but it is better to do that than to brazen out our early declarations when we have at heart faltered in them. There is a decent mean. We can turn our change to account by thinking out what it is and why it is that we once admired and no longer admire ; and we may profitably restrain the emphasis of our new preferences, deciding to wait and see how the new impression wears before we undertake to do critical battle for it.

In advising you thus I am perhaps trying to put a middle-aged head on young shoulders. Youth does not take long views and " hedge " on its opinions ; at least the youth that was I did not spontaneously do so. But I may save you now and then from some stress of unreasonable zeal, or help you here and there to begin to know yourselves—a study that is usually begun rather late in life.

LETTER V

THUS far I have been counselling you as to the moral conditions of right reasoning, on the ground that many, if not most, perversities or fallacies of judgment arise out of faulty states of temper or moral attitudes, or else from lack of the due atmosphere of knowledge, rather than from honest, logical oversight or confusion. By implications, however, we recognise that such honest oversights and confusions are common ; and whether a propounded fallacy be the result of prejudice or of honest error, it may easily happen that an unprejudiced enquirer shall be led astray by it. Let us then look around us for cases of actual fallacy or of bad reasoning, noting how they arise, and how haply we may guard against similar lapses.

First, we have to note the common case of obliviously using terms in different senses. This may happen at times even to a trained reasoner. I find an instance in the procedure of Professor Jevons, the eminent logician, in his little Primer of Political Economy. After defining wealth as consisting in " What is (1) transferable, (2) limited in supply, (3) useful," he goes on to make this observation for the benefit of young readers : " Wealth . . . is far from being the only good thing ; nevertheless it is good, because *it* saves us from too severe labour, from the fear of actual want, and enables us to buy such pleasant things and services as are transferable." Here, you will see, the Professor unwittingly passes from the use of the term wealth in the special sense of his definition—the generality of exchangeable commodities —to the use of it in the ordinary sense, that of individual " riches," the possession or command of a relatively *large share* of economic " wealth." Taken in the first sense, it reduces to nullity the assertion that " it " saves us from too severe labour. The poorest man has some

54

of " it," and the richest has only a portion of " it."
The Professor's " it " is not " wealth " as he had defined
it, but riches—command of a large quantity of wealth
as defined. So again, it is nugatory to say that wealth
as defined " enables us to buy such pleasant things . . .
as are transferable " : the proposition amounts to this,
that wealth enables us to buy wealth.

Still further does the Professor play false to his definition when he proceeds to say that " in a diving-bell or
a deep mine," air, which is usually costless because there
is plenty for all, " becomes limited in supply, and then
may be considered a part of wealth. . . . Even in the
Metropolitan Railway tunnel a little more fresh air
would be truly valuable." The Professor has here for-
gotten the force of the term " transferable " in his own
definition. It there meant " conveyable from one person to another " ; or, more strictly, " from seller to
buyer." Now, there can be no such transfer, no such
conveyance, in the mine, or the diving-bell, or the tunnel.
The railway passenger cannot buy air for use in the
tunnel. The miner or the diver, if working on his own
account, might indeed arrange with someone to pump
air down to him ; but even then he would not be buying the air, he would be buying the services of the
pumper. Air in all these cases, then, is " valuable "
in a sense quite other than that covered by the given
definition of " wealth " ; and to assert its " value " is
as irrelevant to the purpose as to say that pain may
be a valuable discipline.[1]

Here the excessive blundering was probably a result
of sheer failure of attention through fatigue. Professor
Jevons was a very hard worker ; and he presumably
wrote his Primer when his brain was tired. It would
be quite unwarrantable to suppose that he was not concerned to be careful in writing for young readers ; but
perhaps the unwonted need to " talk down " may have
further relaxed his intellectual processes. I incline to

[1] It may have occurred to you that the term " useful " is an
inadequate one for the comprehensive definition of what constitutes
wealth. Diamonds, for instance, rank as wealth, but are not
" useful " in the ordinary sense. " Useful," however, is here taken
in the broad sense of " ministering to desire," and such usage is
permissible. It is essential only that given definitions be adhered
to.

think, however, that in his case there was some natural lack of the capacity to use words accurately and easily. He has told that he found it impossible to learn German, for want of linguistic gift ; and though one rarely finds the specially good linguists to be deep thinkers, it may be that an abnormal shortcoming in the power to learn a foreign language is a phase of some congenital defect of verbal faculty in general.

This, at least, seems the only excuse for the lapses from logical statement which occur even in Mr. Jevons's most careful performances. For instance, in his essay on *The Substitution of Similars* he has this sentence :

> These laws may seem *truisms*, and they were ridiculed as such by Locke ; *but*, since they describe the very nature of identity in its three aspects, they *must be assumed as true*, consciously or unconsciously ; and if we can build a system of inference upon them, their self-evidence is surely in our favour.[1]

Here the " but " is absurd : a truism is a self-evident proposition, that is the meaning of the word ; and from such a proposition no logical " inference " can be drawn. Aristotle framed the formula, " A is either B or not B," in order to bar the triflers who were capable of saying that it might be both. But that admission is merely a condition precedent for all rational discussion ; it cannot yield an " inference," since it leaves all real propositions untouched.

Let me now give you, from the same work of Professor Jevons, a paragraph constituting an entirely fallacious argument on a question of practical politics. When you have analysed it, you will be partly experienced in one mode of confused reasoning :

> At the present day . . . the Government is called upon to take charge of the telegraphs and railways, because great benefit has resulted from their [its] management of the post-office. It is implied in this demand that the telegraphs and railways resemble or are even identical with the post-office in those points which render Government control beneficial. . . . The whole question turns, of course, upon the degree and particular nature of the similarity. Granting that there is sufficient analogy between the telegraph and the post-office to render the Government purchase of the former desirable, we *must not favour* so gigantic an enterprise as the purchase of the railways until it is clearly made out that their successful management depends upon principles of economy exactly similar to the case of the post-office.[2]

---

[1] Essay cited, pp. 46–7.   [2] Work cited, p. 72.

You have already noted, I hope, the illicit procedure. To begin with, it was *not* implied in the appeal in question that the main points of management of railways were " identical " with those of the post-office. The argument was : " We have done the one ; we may do the other." To say, then, that we " must not favour " the appeal until the principles of successful management are proved to be " exactly similar " is to affirm a plain *non-sequitur*. We may fitly favour the appeal for many reasons. All that properly follows is : " We must not *ground* our demand for railway nationalisation on the mere success of the post-office until we have shown that the enterprises would have substantially the same economic or financial conditions." Here again we seem to be dealing with a want of faculty for statement ; and I incline to think that Mr. Jevons's love for symbolic forms of argument, and for his " logical abacus," was correlative with this shortcoming. Symbols, it is conceivable, may be specially helpful to a thinker who is awkward in the use of words ; and I have more than once noticed skill in or proclivity to the use of them in men who were either normally or chronically slow of speech, or slow at sentence formation and syntax.

Far be it from me, however, to suggest that the glib-tongued men are usually accurate reasoners. What I mean is that Jevons had a large part of the outfit or structure of a good reasoner, but miscarried because of one congenital defect. Many a fluent man has neither the gift of coherence nor the concern to acquire it ; and if a slow-tongued professor of logic yields you samples of spurious argument, eloquent politicians will probably yield you a good many more.

Another case of covert transformation of terms, to the detriment of the argument, occurs in the work of that very gifted scholar and anthropologist, the late Professor Robertson Smith, on *The Religion of the Semites*. On page 55 he writes :

It is not with a vague fear of unknown powers, but with a loving reverence for *known Gods* who are knit to their worshippers by strong bonds of kinship, that religion *in the only true sense of the word* begins. Religion *in this sense* is not the child of terror ; and the difference between it and the savage's dread of unseen foes is as absolute and fundamental in the *earliest* as in the latest stages of development.

In the next chapter (p. 88), apparently forgetting altogether that he had written as above, he writes :

> The immediate inference from all this is that the origins of Semitic, and indeed of all antique *religion*, go back to a stage of human thought in which the question of the nature of the Gods, as distinguished from other beings, did not even arise in any precise form, *because no one series of existences was strictly differentiated from another*.

That this inference is his permanent or normal position we may gather from pp. 27, 88, and other passages. Thus the passage first above cited is a flat contradiction of his general teaching. The second passage, however, is in turn contradicted by one on p. 129, where it is asserted that " the transformation of certain groups of hostile demons into friendly and kindred powers " is " already effected, by means of totemism, in the *most primitive* societies of savages "—there is contradiction, that is, unless the writer means " savages *now* existing." But he proceeds to assert that " there is no record of a stage in human society in which each community of men did not claim *kindred and alliance* with *some* group or species of the living powers of nature."

The inconsistency in the latter case is one that might arise through mere over-readiness to generalise emphatically. The generaliser, like the general liar, had need have a good memory. But the glaring contradiction of the two first-cited passages is to be traced, I think, back to the old moral infirmity which we have already considered. Professor Robertson Smith was a professional theologian first and an anthropologist afterwards ; and his outburst about " religion in the only true sense of the word " appears to have been an expression of his carnal resentment of the attitude of rationalists who rejected his theology altogether. In this state of temper he was capable of giving as the " only true sense " of religion one which he himself usually rejected, as he affirms it only in this passage. After the passage cited from p. 55 he categorically asserts that " It is only in times of social dissolution, as in the last age of the small Semitic states . . . that magical superstitions based on mere terror . . . invade the sphere of tribal or national religion." In the passage cited from p. 129 he asserts on the contrary that such superstitions are immeasurably early.

Of such an exhibition we are entitled to speak strongly. It proves that the writer's prejudice made him " insincere " and *ad hoc* unscrupulous ; and if we studied only such aspects of his work we should be led to think him an extremely untrustworthy and indeed incompetent reasoner. But this he was not. Where his theological prepossessions did not come into play he was an acute and original thinker ; and the first lesson of his lapses is that which I have already urged on you —that we must be constantly on the watch against our emotional leanings if we would be faithful and just reasoners. But there is further to be kept in view the risk that we may without prejudice fall into other men's errors if we read them without constant critical attention. Be not such readers, I beg of you. One book critically read yields more education than twenty skimmed inattentively. Those who so read Robertson Smith as to be satisfied equally with his original and scientific thinking on the psychology of ancient sacrificial rites, and with his fulminations of pulpit claptrap, have substantially failed to profit by him. His lectures on Semitic religion, remember, were originally delivered to audiences of church-going people—that is to say, in an atmosphere stimulative and evocative of claptrap. It takes an uncommon degree of intellectual scrupulosity to save a man from ever saying on a popular platform things that are below the standard of critical taste which he recognises at his desk.

Even at the desk, however, a professed expert may blunder grievously under the spur of temper. The late Professor Momerie, who held the chair of Logic and Metaphysics in King's College, London, published a little book *On Belief in God*, which was praised as " wise " and " philosophic " by certain reviewers of his own way of thinking. At the outset he founds on the (alleged) universality of the " desire for God " as affording a strong presumption, though not a proof, of the existence of a Supernatural Person. The absence of " the religious sentiments," he asserts, " is exceptional and rare." Yet in the same chapter, growing visibly angry over the suggestion that advance in culture will raise men

above theism as they have been raised above polytheism, he writes : " Agnostic opinions, I admit, are
rapidly gaining acceptance among the multitude ; but
this is just because agnosticism is essentially shallow
and superficial, and therefore very easily mastered."
Not only does he thus contradict his opening proposition :
he expressly disparages the thinking of the multitude
as being shallow and superficial, in the act of maintaining the thesis that an opinion of the multitude is likely
to turn out sound.   Here we have a flagrant insincerity,
plainly attributable to temper, on the part of one whose
special business it was to transcend the snares of temper.
And other educated men, sharing his animosities, fail to
detect his self-contradiction even when it is their special
business to do so.

I seem always to return, thus far, to my original
warnings against the moral snares in the path of the
reasoner.   Can it be, I wonder, that fallacies arise even
more often through temper and prejudice than I had
supposed ?   Howsoever that may be, the next sample of
inconsistent reasoning that occurs to me is in Hegel ;
and I fancy we shall have to revert even in his case
to the moral mode of explanation.   Arguing for his proposition that all History is the process of the universal
Reason, he writes :

It was for a while the fashion to profess admiration for the
wisdom of God as displayed in animals, plants, and isolated occurrences. . . .   Why not also in Universal History ?   But Divine
Wisdom—*i.e.*, Reason, is one and the same in the great as in the
little. . . .[1]

Yet only a few lines above he had written : " God
wishes no narrow-hearted souls or empty heads for his
children ; but those whose spirit is of itself indeed poor,
but rich in the knowledge of Him."   I have never met
with a Hegelian who would undertake to reconcile this
foolish sentence with such a proposition as that cited
above.   In that, Hegel affirms the universal immanence
of what he calls " God."   In this he speaks of his God
as a vaunting soldier might speak of his General, or
as any vulgar person might wrangle with any other concerning his own merits or procedure.   But Hegel was
certainly not a mere braggart or vulgarian : he was a

[1] *Philosophy of History*, Eng. trans., p. 16.

man of singular originality and depth of thought, however often he may " maunder," as one of his disciples
says he does. For the explanation of an imbecility on
his part, then, we must look either in his temper or in
some failure of due knowledge.

In many cases he was absurd because he arrogantly
insisted that he could know facts in nature *a priori* :
there temper and ignorance combined to make him
miscarry extravagantly. Here the trouble is simply
temper. He has set out to rebut " the doctrine that
it is impossible to know God " ; and on this errand he
passes from one form of insolence to another. First,
he asserts that if we make the affirmation he challenges
we " have the convenient licence of wandering as far
as we list in the direction of our own fancies "—a suggestion that the men he opposes are seeking a philosophy which shall leave no restraints on their actions.
This is the method of the lowest order of theologian :
it would be difficult to reason more ignobly, more con-
temptibly. To attribute your opponent's alleged but
unproved error to a criminal motive which is peculiar to
him, is to make an end of the conditions of argument
between you and him. There is all the difference of two
stages of civilisation between such a fashion of initially
ascribing your adversary's views to bad character, and
the process of first showing him to be in error and then
surmising that he erred through emotional bias.

By way of fulminating the more effectually against his
philosophic foes, Hegel proceeds in the passage in question to profess that, while their philosophy is heterodox,
he is orthodox. " In the Christian religion," he writes,
" God has revealed Himself—that is, He has given us
to understand what He is ; so that He is no longer a concealed or secret existence." There are many grounds for
believing that this was not even an honest expression of
Hegel's belief. And it is after this that he explodes as
above noted against the " narrow-hearted souls or empty
heads " ; an utterance opposed alike to Christian doctrine, Hegelian philosophy, common-sense, and good
manners, its aim being simply to asperse those who
held another view of things than the Hegelian.

When we turn from the outbreak of temper to the
doctrine it aims at vindicating, we are presumably on

higher ground. Inconsistency in argument, as I have urged, is a proof of " insincerity " ; but when we come to a main thesis, whether or not it be consistent with the other positions of its framer, we have to reckon with it as the expression of a deliberated thought. And Hegel's formula of History is a main item in his philosophy, which laudably strove to reach a unified and all-sufficing notion of the universe. Here we have an exercise on the higher levels of reasoning.

Let us ask ourselves, first, what we are to understand by Hegel's reiterated theorem, or theorems, that Reason rules the universe, " That Reason is the Sovereign of the World ; that the history of the world, therefore, presents us with a rational process "; that " Reason is the substance of the Universe " ; that " it reveals itself in the world, and that in that world nothing else is revealed but this and its honour and glory " ; that, finally, the history of the world " has constituted the rational necessary course of the World Spirit." What is here really meant ? Hegel goes on to declare that the laws of cosmic movement " *are* Reason, implicit in the phenomena in question " ; but, of course, adds that the cosmic bodies are not conscious. Soon he proceeds to say that " Reason is thought conditioning itself with perfect freedom " ; and his reconciliation of this with the notion of Reason as implicit in phenomena—in the movements of unconscious bodies—seems to consist in saying that there is a fundamental distinction between an abstract principle and its " determinate application and concrete development." But in the same page he says that " Divine Providence is Wisdom, endowed with an infinite Power, which realises its aim—viz. the absolute rational design of the world " ; and in the next, after some inconclusive reflection, he tells us that " our earnest endeavour must be directed to the recognition of the ways of Providence, the means it uses, and the historical phenomena in which it manifests itself." It is after this that he breaks out as aforesaid about God's wishing no narrow-hearted souls or empty heads for his children.

Here, despite the dialectic advantage derived by Hegel from sheer laxity of expression—the advantage, that is, of keeping us in hesitation as to his meaning—it becomes finally clear that he has committed in his whole argument thus far the self-contradiction reached in that explosion about God's wishes.

He makes cosmic Reason alternately the process of events and a force directing events (" Reason *directs* the world " is one of his phrases : " Reason is the *substance* of the Universe," is another) ; and after laying it down that every event is " providential " he tells us to recognise the " ways of Providence," a proposition which either limits those ways to special orders of phenomena or amounts to the mere nullity that we ought to recognise what we perceive. This contradiction he seeks, as it were, to brazen out when he goes on to say that he is undertaking " a justification of the ways of God . . . so that the ill that is found in the world may be comprehended, and the thinking Spirit reconciled with the fact of the existence of evil." And how does he propose to effect the reconciliation ? In the only way possible, he says ; that way being " by recognising the *positive* existence, in which that negative element is a subordinate and vanquished nullity." Try to imagine a " vanquished nullity " ; and then ask yourselves why there was any need to trouble about reconciling the discord of a vanquished nullity with " the thinking spirit." " Evil," says the philosopher, " has not been able permanently to assert a competing position." Has not been able ! This, after we have learned that Reason directs the whole world ; that all acts are rational acts and divine acts ; that in the world " nothing is revealed but reason and its honour and glory." What then *is* this Evil which is a nullity, and cannot permanently compete, and yet is an expression of Reason, and nevertheless needs to be reconciled with Spirit ? Does the philosopher believe what he has been saying ?

At this critical point he avows that " an adequate definition of Reason is the first desideratum . . . without such a definition we get no further than mere words." It is most true ; and the avowal reminds us that we are in presence of a strenuous effort to *think* the universe into an order, to comprehend it, to explain it. Terms have been transformed, definitions outraged, far more seriously than we saw to be the case in the

cited passages of Jevons and Robertson Smith ; but
the psychology of the process seems to be different.
Hegel is vehemently struggling all the while with his
problem : his incoherences of phrase are the expression
of his difficulty. But the more clearly we realise his
absorption, the intensity of his desire, the pressure of
his conviction that it all *must* be explicable, the more
clearly, I think, do we feel that his quest is vain. He
is in the toils of an insoluble enigma, and his desire to
solve it can no more avail than the Will-to-Live can
make us immortal. The passion to solve the enigma,
we begin to see, is one of the lures of life. Hegel *would*
not give up the quest : here he is on all fours with the
theosophist of all ages ; and, where others affect to
have revelations, he doggedly insists with himself to
the last that his intuition must take form in a reasoned
demonstration.

Inevitably the further demonstration is a repeated
movement in a circle. "What," he asks, " is the ultimate design of the World ? " and he works out a fresh
formula : " The final cause of the World at large is the
consciousness of its own freedom on the part of Spirit."
The next question is : By what means is this consciousness reached ? and at once we are launched on a
theorem which, instead of presenting us with a pervading Reason, gives us the " World-Spirit " as proceeding through " Unreason," evil, ruin, corruption,
decay. Still he insists on finding a rational purpose ;
and once more he readjusts his struggling thought,
avowing that " Principle, Plan of Existence, Law, is a
hidden, undeveloped essence, which *as such*, however
true in itself, is not completely real." It becomes real,
that is to say, through Will, human passion, desire,
action ; and it is admitted that " the history of mankind does not begin with a conscious aim of any kind."
Yet it is in the history of mankind alone that Spirit, in
this theory, can realise itself ; so that the " plan " of
absolute " Reason " *is* simply the slow emergence of an
ideal in evolving man ; and its absolute " Freedom " is
nothing more than the human consciousness of aspiration
and of personality. And now, after the express undertaking to show Evil as a vanquished nullity, we have
this smashing confession : " The History of the World

is not the theatre of happiness. Periods of happiness are blank pages in it, for they are periods of harmony, periods when the antithesis is in abeyance."

Just here, however, Hegel grasps a conception which seems to him to yield him his justification. Even as wind and water lend themselves to the making of iron and the working of wood which form a house that will keep out wind and water ; and even as the gravity of stones, their tendency to fall, makes possible the wall which rises high and remains firm, so do the passions of men " build up the edifice of human society, thus fortifying a position for Right and Order against themselves." But here, in the very flight of verbal triumph, the collapse of the thesis is plain ; for the upbuilding alleged is in terms of the case conditioned by the hostile forces ; the house is there only because of the forces of downfall, which never cease their attack ; the fortress of Right and Order must in the terms of the case be for ever besieged ; and as the assault must be capable of partial or chronic success if the alleged process is not to be a farce, the Evil is no vanquished nullity, but an eternal element in the " scheme " of things.

We are left with the familiar theistic sophism that Evil is right because it is the condition of the existence of Good ; a proposition maintained by the very mouths which most wrathfully denounce Evil. They do but brazen out their insoluble problem. Hegel must do as much throughout his philosophy of history ; must condemn, indict, expose ; must, in short, exhibit the World-Spirit—which was to be proven Good, Reason, Freedom realising itself—as the mere totality of human action, whereof the imperfection is always driving the theosophist to frame schemes in which the Order that was to be vindicated and explained is to vanish and be superseded by a perfect one that in the terms of the whole discussion will be unthinkable, because its Good will not be made recognisable by Evil !

I shall not attempt further to expound and criticise Hegel for you : I am trying to help you to reason, not to supply you with a rounded philosophy. But at least you will catch the drift of my exposition—that Hegel is caught in his own net ; that where some men commit fallacy by force of commonplace prejudice, or the oversight of fatigue, or inadequate reasoning faculty, he commits it in virtue of an intense intuition that the solution of the infinite problem is within his reach, and that he can somehow beat out that solution in words. In the face of such an ardent aspiration the ignoble insolences which we first considered are partially excusable : we see, at least, that they are not the gist of Hegel's exposition. But do not forget that to such insolences the argument comes when it attempts to meet the rebuttals of its procedure.

An accomplished Hegelian, to whom I once observed that Hegel's pronouncements on practical issues—such as those of politics and current religion—were always those of quite unphilosophic men, and never in accord with his philosophy, answered in terms of one of Hegel's own avowals, that in the all-thinking philosopher himself there is a simple " John Smith," a man of common passions, who has his say in the philosopher's name. It is verily so ; but I have never been able to understand how the avowal could content a Hegelian. In any case, it corroborates the position I have so frequently taken up in these letters, that emotion dictates, if not most, certainly far too many of our reasonings. And though so intense a preoccupation as Hegel's seems almost to exclude the notion that in his case there can have been any of that " insincerity " on which I have so often insisted, there is no escape at least from the reflection that we ourselves will do well to put the challenge of that conception to even the most intense of our own presuppositions if we find that our reasonings in support of them are not at every joint impenetrable to the sharpest pressures of the test of consistency.

I need hardly point out to you in so many words that Hegel's miscarriage is reducible to an identification of his own mental processes with the infinite process of the Universe. There is this justification for his calling the infinite process " reason," that it becomes significant for us only as a process of causation, a perpetual " therefore," an endless chain of " becauses." Such a chain is our reason. But we merely addle our heads with words when we jump to the notion that, even as our reason is a perpetual tracing of " therefores," so the causation of things in all Nature amounts to the sequence of therefores in an infinite Reason. Reason is too weak a process of bead-stringing, when all is said, to be without puerility likened to an inconceivable totality of which we can but say negatively that it is no mere sequence, but infinite in all directions, infinite *qua* co-existences as well as *qua* sequences—that is to say, not totally a " sequence " at all, since sequence is but an expression of relativity.

Hegel, indeed, as we have seen, strikes down his own truth in his effort to transcend the absolute. What we have to learn, as the total lesson of Nature, is that every human experience, like every state of natural objects, is a result, of which it is our business to know the order, item by item. Error and evil, delusion and crime and madness, are to be so envisaged, if we would rationally face life : we must understand them in order to correct or exclude them in future. But if we begin to define them as aspects of an Infinite Reason, parts of the plan of a Divine Wisdom, we shall either paralyse our every test, and stultify our corrective purpose, or else relapse into that theological irrationalism which yields the maximum of cruelty in human affairs, since it reconciles men to the deliberate infliction of misery by way of punishing an evil that in the terms of the argument is willed and wrought by Divine Goodness. Of that negation of reason Hegel, I fear, was not incapable.

We have repeatedly come, in this last discussion, to the terminology of theism : Hegel's doctrine of Reason in history being, in fact, a way of approaching and handling the theistic problem. That problem is so likely to meet you often in life that I am fain to lead you to it on each and all of the many lines on which it is commonly approached, hoping so to shorten somewhat for you the processes of dialectic which stand between us and clear conclusions on the matter. But I shall be doing you little service if I do not set you re-thinking every one of my steps, checking my chain of therefores, and finally looking at the problem with your own eyes, seeking light for yourselves wherever you find me obscure or unsatisfying. In other letters we shall approach the problem on other lines of argument. If I am helping you at all, you will find the pilgrimage not uninteresting. At the time I write these letters for your future reading, you being far too young to understand them, you daily tackle me with countless comical " whys." I would fain hope that when you read these pages you will be as comprehensive in your curiosity, practising, however, on your own faculties as you used to hammer at mine.

WE have seen how even a trained logician like the late Professor Jevons, working with a formal definition in a treatise that aimed at scientifically exact statement, could lose sight of his own chosen terms and thus seriously confuse his argument, even when he was not swayed by any prejudice. Unless, then, formal logic positively miseducates men for argument, great must be the likelihood of such confusion on the part of fluent writers who venture on long processes of argument, over complex issues, without any trained sense of the difficulties of exact reasoning. Especially great are their logical risks when their argument deals, so to speak, with the very stuff of argument, the processes of thought and feeling which constitute opinion.

A notable instance lies to hand in a very interesting work, which you will do well to read—the *History of the Rise and Influence of the Spirit of Rationalism in Europe*, by Mr. W. E. H. Lecky. I must warn you that Mr. Lecky, though an industrious, is a somewhat careless historian. He has done good service in bringing together much interesting information on the history of opinion ; and he is usually to be trusted when he gives details for which he cites his authorities. When, however, he offers general statements on processes of development prior to those which he treats at length, he is at times extravagantly wrong. The assertion, for instance, concerning Averroïsm, that " the teachings of a stern and uncompromising infidelity flashed forth from Seville and Cordova," [1] is utterly misleading ; and no less so is the proposition that " In the towns, paganism had arrived at the last stage of decrepitude when Christianity arose ; and therefore in the towns the victory of Christianity was prompt and decisive." [2] A " victory " which

[1] Work cited, ed. 1887, i., 48.   [2] *Id.*, p. 36.

took three hundred years to accomplish is not plausibly to be called " prompt " ; and the writer's own context implies that it was not " decisive," inasmuch as " the different elements of paganism continued to exist in a transfigured form, and under new names."

But what I want now to discuss with you is the intellectual confusion revealed in the preface to Mr. Lecky's work. It is, I think, purely a matter of fallacy —that is to say, there is no moral bias at work. He sets out, as I understand him, to maintain a proposition nearly identical with one I have suggested to you in a previous letter—namely, that beliefs and arguments which to men at a certain stage of knowledge are plausible and convincing, are by men of fuller knowledge seen at a glance to be worthless. The point is that when we get to know a mass of the most relevant *facts* bearing upon an erroneous traditional belief, we readily dispose of it by arguments which could not be thought of by those who had not those facts before them, and had to deal with the belief, as it were, *in vacuo*. Mr. Lecky's logical mishaps occur in his effort to state this proposition in terms of the psychological processes of normal conviction.

When [he writes] towards the close of the eighteenth century the decline of theological passions enabled men to discuss these [theological] matters in a calmer spirit, and when increased knowledge produced more comprehensive views . . . it was observed that every great change of belief had been preceded by a great change in the intellectual condition of Europe ; that the success of any opinion depended much less upon the force of its arguments, or upon the abilities of its advocates, than upon the predisposition of society to receive it, and that that predisposition resulted from the intellectual type of the age. As men advance from an imperfect to a higher civilisation they gradually sublimate and refine their creed. . . .

The pressure of the general intellectual influences of the time determines the predispositions which ultimately regulate the details of the belief. . . . A change of speculative opinion does not imply an increase of the data upon which those opinions rest, but a change of the habits of thought and mind which they reflect. Definite arguments are the symptoms and pretexts, but seldom the causes of the change. Their chief merit is to accelerate the inevitable crisis. They derive their force and efficacy from their conformity with the mental habits of those to whom they are addressed. Reasoning which in one age would make no impression whatever, in the next age is received with enthusiastic applause.

Thus far the confusion consists in a failure to assign

fixed values to terms. What Mr. Lecky ought to have said in the second of the sentences above quoted is that every great change of belief had been preceded by many smaller changes *of belief*. He writes of " intellectual condition " and " intellectual influences " as if these were not in terms of beliefs. Obviously they are. Instead therefore of saying that pressure of general intellectual influences determines a predisposition which determines beliefs (that is what Mr. Lecky's loose phrasing comes to), one should say that beliefs on great or central issues are prepared or determined by beliefs on smaller issues.

How, then, are those minor beliefs so altered as to affect major beliefs ? We must answer, Either by simple definite argument or by presentments of fact which evoke and clinch definite argument. To say that definite arguments merely " accelerate the inevitable crisis " is a fresh confusion. There can be no " crisis " until definite arguments are forthcoming. What Mr. Lecky should have said is that definite arguments of an innovating kind on a great or central issue have to be preceded by definite arguments on minor issues if they are to be made acceptable. " Mental habits " are substantially habits of belief. The result of this initial obscurity in Mr. Lecky's thinking is that, with the truth under his eyes, he falls into a definite self-contradiction.

This tone and habit of thought [he proceeds] is created, not by the influences arising out of any one department of intellect, but by the combination of all the intellectual and even social tendencies of the age. *Those who contribute most largely to its formation are*, I believe, *the philosophers*. Men like Bacon, Descartes, and Locke have probably done more than any others to set the current of their age. *They* have formed a certain cast and tone of mind. They have *introduced* peculiar habits of thought, new modes of reasoning, new tendencies of enquiry.

Here, you will see, the original idea is completely lost sight of. What the philosophers deal in are precisely the " definite arguments " which the writer has told us are " the symptoms and pretexts, but seldom the causes, of the change." If the philosophers can successfully " *introduce* peculiar habits of thought, new modes of reasoning," all the foregoing argument comes to nothing. The " conformity with the mental habits of those to whom they are addressed," above declared to be necessary, has disappeared. If a single writer can for his own time " form a certain cast and tone of mind," what is the meaning of the assertion that " a change of speculative opinions " implies " a change of the habits of thought and mind which they reflect " ? How came the innovating philosopher to innovate ?

The tangle is to be unravelled by going back to the truth obscured at the start. Important changes of opinion, or changes in important opinion, whether on the part of individuals or of numbers, are the result of minor changes of opinion, or changes in minor opinions. Not that any one minor change is necessarily primary in a given process : many minor opinions may be revolutionised as the result of a great change ; but the point is that no great change of belief occurs save as a result of a number of smaller mental adaptations—that is, changes of belief. Mr. Lecky, casting back towards his escaped proposition, proceeds to say : " But philosophical methods, *great* and unquestionable as is their power, form *but one of the many* influences that contribute to the mental habits of society." To say that a " great " influence is " but one of many " is to misuse language. The " many " cannot all be " great " : the more items there are in a given total, the less great are they relatively. And Mr. Lecky proceeds to give illustrations which, while they will help you to see what he is driving at, do not help out either of the last-cited propositions.

Thus the discoveries of physical science, encroaching upon the domain of the anomalous and the incomprehensible, enlarging our conceptions of the reign of law, and revealing the connection of phenomena that had formerly appeared altogether isolated, form a habit of mind which is carried far beyond the limits of physics. Thus the astronomical discovery that our world is not the centre and axis of the material universe, but is an inconsiderable planet . . . revolving with many others around a sun which is itself but an infinitesimal point in creation [Mr. Lecky means " in the universe "] . . . has a vast and palpable influence upon our theological conceptions.

If this be so, the " vast " influence is primarily exerted not by a philosopher's " new mode of reasoning " but by the impact of a realised truth—a belief—on beliefs seen to be correlative with that. [In point of fact, the belief in question has only very gradually affected the theological doctrines on which it properly bears : its influence, therefore, was not speedily " palpable," and it is not even now " vast " as regards the majority of religious people ; but we must agree that it ought logically to be very great.]

Mr. Lecky now proceeds to a fresh inconsequence. If his views be correct, he says,

they establish at once a broad distinction between the province of the theologian and that of the historian of opinions. . . . The first is restricted to a single department of mental phenomena, and to those logical connections which determine the opinions of the severe reasoner ; the second is obliged to take a wide survey of the intellectual influences of the period he is describing, and to trace that connection of congruity which has a much greater influence upon the sequence of opinions than logical arguments.

Here we come upon the old fallacy as to what constitutes a logical argument. It is quite true that there is a broad distinction between the theologian as such and the historian of opinion ; but it is not of the sort that Mr. Lecky suggests. The theologian's business is to theologise, to state and argue his creed on lines of " revelation " or of *a priori* assumption and deduction ; the business of the historian of opinion is to show when, how, and why theological and other opinions were commonly formed and altered. But " connection of congruity " is an aspect of the exposition of both ; and it is a gratuitous error to drive the historian of opinion off the ground of " logical argument," though Mr. Lecky in a sense is not exactly at home there. The theologian, indeed, is practically driven to take note of the very facts in culture-history to which the historian points as explaining changes in theological opinion, and to try to accommodate those facts to his theology, or it to them, in terms of " connection of congruity."

At this point Mr. Lecky diverges to the great question of free-will, the discussion of which I reserve for another letter : in the meantime let us follow him on his return to the matters above considered. Here he will again serve you as an object lesson in reasoning.

Nothing [he writes] can be more certain to an attentive observer than that the great majority even of those who reason much about their opinions have arrived at their conclusions by a process quite distinct from reasoning. They may be perfectly unconscious of the fact, but the ascendancy of old associations is upon them ; and, in the overwhelming majority of cases, men of the most various creeds conclude their investigations by simply acquiescing in the opinions they have been taught.

The last statement is, I think, perfectly true. Professor Bain, for his part, remarking on the " strong probability that any given individual has never exercised any independent judgment in politics or in religion," declares that a " hundred to one is a safe estimate of such a probability." [1] But this is not the same thing as saying that most " even of those who reason much about their opinions have arrived at their conclusions by *a process quite distinct from reasoning.*" Observe Professor Bain's circumspect phrase : " Any *independent* judgment " : he does not say " any judgment." Any " investigation " *is* a process of reasoning. What Mr. Lecky should have said is that the processes of reasoning of most people are incomplete, short-sighted, relatively " uncritical," uncandid. As I have tried to show you, there is a heavy presumption that our errors of reasoning may be traced to faulty moods, to prejudice, to temper, to hasty belief in propositions of fact ; but none the less the process of error is a process of reasoning. Error is a mode of judgment : broadly speaking, it is an incomplete process of judgment.

This holds good, obviously, of errors which are not mere echoings of one's teachers. As Mr. Lecky himself puts it, " the love of singularity, the ambition to be thought intellectually superior to others, the bias of taste, the attraction of vice, the influence of friendship, the magnetism of genius—these, and *countless other influences* . . . all determine conclusions." He is describing the case of " those who have *diverged from* the opinions they had been taught " ; and he here implies that they are many ; but again he is confused, for the influences of friendship and genius are forms of " teaching." He then goes on :

The number of persons who have a *rational basis* for their belief is probably infinitesimal ; for illegitimate influences not only determine the convictions of those who do not examine, but usually give a dominating bias to the reasonings of those who do. But it would be manifestly absurd to conclude from this that reason has no part or function in the formation of opinions.

[1] *Induction*, 2nd ed., p. 136.

Quite so, you will say with me. I think that Mr. Lecky would have done better *not* to assert the absurdity as he actually did, when he is thus forced to unsay his dictum. " All that we can rightly infer is," he continues, " that the process of reasoning is much more difficult than is commonly supposed." Precisely ! The pity is that Mr. Lecky did not at this stage profit by the discovery, to the extent of recasting his preface. Just after the avowal he repeats without hesitation his formula that " the *opinions* of a given period are mainly determined by the *intellectual condition* of society " ; as if opinions in general were not elements in the intellectual condition.

We begin to suspect an inaptitude for right statement on Mr. Lecky's part when we find him going on thus :

Those who have appreciated the extremely small influence of definite arguments in determining the opinions either of an individual or of a nation—who have perceived how invariably an increase of civilisation implies a modification of belief, and how completely the controversialists of successive ages are the puppets and the unconscious exponents of the deep under-current of their time, will feel an intense distrust of their unassisted reason, and will naturally look for some guide to direct their judgment. I think it must be admitted that the general and increasing tendency in the present day is to seek such a guide in the *collective wisdom of mankind* as it is displayed in the developments of history. *In other words*, the way in which our leading thinkers, consciously or unconsciously, form their opinions is by endeavouring to ascertain what are the laws that govern the successive modifications of belief.

It is quite true that a study of the strenuous error of past thinkers may fitly set up in us a distrust of our *unassisted* reason : that is to say, seeing how many false beliefs have been fiercely held because of ignorance of the relevant facts, we are moved to seek on all hands for knowledge on which to build our opinions. But to say that we find a guide in the " collective wisdom of mankind," and that that wisdom is " displayed in the developments of history," is to use glaring misnomers. What constitutes " the collective wisdom of mankind " it is very hard to say ; but certainly there is nothing plausibly to be so called in the mere process of change. Past error is the collective *un*wisdom of mankind : present beliefs, in terms of the very doctrine of develop-

ment, are to be suspected at every point ; and many
of those held by the largest numbers are, in the opinion
of minorities, as false as any of the past. To " assist "
your reason you turn, not to the beliefs of mankind
in mass, but to the reasonings and researches of the
studious few. It is only they who can—at least it is
only they who do—think out " the laws that govern
the successive modifications of belief."

Broadly speaking, these laws are : that men tend to
believe (1) as they were taught ; (2) as their economic
interests lie ; (3) as their knowledge guides them. The
last-named factor of necessity operates slowly, knowledge beginning with the few, and only with difficulty
reaching the many. To realise this is not to be impressed by the collective wisdom of mankind. Where
interests can be directly and forcibly affected, opinion
will be affected : thus in the English Reformation the
processes of plunder which revolted some made staunch
Protestants of others—those who profited by the plunder.
They became highly receptive to arguments that formerly
they would have rejected. But where new doctrines do
not set up or are not helped by an economic interest
—where they have against them both vested interests
and established teaching, their fortune is of the hardest.
The collective wisdom of mankind, in this aspect, is a
very poor affair.

Mr. Lecky would probably admit all this ; but his
careless reasoning never lets it clearly appear. He speaks
of the developments of science and philosophy and in-
dustrial life as going on " till the period when conclusions [which] the reason had once naturally and almost
instinctively adopted seem incongruous and grotesque "
—here admitting after all that wrong beliefs are reached
and held by way of reasoning—and then puts his case
thus :

When an opinion that is *opposed to the age* is incapable of modification, and is an obstacle to progress, it will at last be openly
repudiated ; and if it is identified with any existing interests, or
associated with some eternal truth, its rejection will be accompanied
by paroxysms of painful agitation. But much more frequently
civilisation makes opinions that are opposed to it simply obsolete.
They perish by indifference, not by controversy. They are relegated
to the dim twilight land that surrounds every living faith ; the
land of the unrealised and the inoperative.

I commend this to your notice as a sample of how you ought *not* to write or talk on sociological questions : a sample of the muddle of notions that may result from the free movement of a rhetorical style. First " an opinion that is opposed to the age " is the loosest of descriptions. It may fitly be applied to a *new* opinion, a disturbing doctrine, such as were the theories of Copernicus and Newton and Laplace and Darwin and the geologists when they were first put forth. Yet Mr. Lecky means by his phrase " an old or established opinion which is inconsistent with a number of recently acquired opinions." By " some eternal truth " he means " religious belief," and the proposition would be as true if he had written " popular delusion." He speaks, finally, of opinions that perish, yet do not perish, being relegated to the " land of the unrealised and inoperative." He might have placed in that landscape a good many opinions that are professedly held as sacred—for instance, the saying that we ought to love our neighbour as ourselves.

Of what was he thinking ? Let us turn to his book for light. He says in the preface :

> My object in the present work has been to trace the history of the spirit of Rationalism ; by which I understand, not any class of definite doctrines or criticisms, but rather a certain cast of thought, or bias of reasoning, which has during the last three centuries gained a marked ascendancy in Europe. The nature of this bias will be exhibited in the ensuing pages, when we examine its influence upon the various forms of moral and intellectual development.

It turns out, however, that he *does* deal with quite a number of definite doctrines and criticisms, and that he has *not* followed the effect of the rationalistic cast of thought in its length and breadth. The word Rationalist has had a notable history. In Germany, about 1600, it was applied (1) to certain Aristotelian humanists at Helmstadt by their opponents. In England, in Bacon's day, it was applied to (2) the physicists who proceeded on *a priori* theory in disregard of experience. During the Civil War, it was applied to (3) a small sect or group who professed to " follow reason " in their religion and their politics. A little later, we find it applied to Unitarians and Deists. About the end of the seventeenth century and in the first quarter of the eighteenth, it

signified one of those Christians who claimed to give
rational grounds for their religious tenets. Those applications having disappeared from common usage, a century later the name Rationalism was commonly applied
to the critical method of certain li
Germany, who, following a method s
Peyrere and the English Toland, so
explanations of miracle-stories in
terms of the case, it was not of th
Rationalism that Mr. Lecky seeks t
nor even of the last, though he gla
save when he is dealing with such
as that of recovered pagan art on
naissance, his own pages constantly
arguments " played a great part i
notes.

In his opening chapter, for instanc
belief in magic and witchcraft, and
himself makes it partly evident that
served in turn to promote, to mainta
it. There was a whole library of
propagate the belief in the later Mid
admitted that, at a time when free
could not safely be printed, the fr
faces against it.[1] There must thei
great deal of definite argument before Montaigne avowed
his unbelief ; and he in turn, by Mr. Lecky's admission,[2] met the superstition by " a mode of argument
which was destined long afterwards to assume a most
prominent place in theological controversy "—the argument, namely, used by Hume against miracles, that it
is more likely that men's senses or their testimony
should err than that the normally recognised laws of
Nature should be violated. To say of Montaigne that
" the bent and character of his mind led him to believe
that witchcraft was grossly improbable "—thus giving
the whole credit to his special genius—is to misstate the
historical facts. In his youth he was both credulous
and fanatical ; and it was only after many years of
painfully educative experience that, recoiling alike from
Catholic and Protestant fanaticism, he became broadly

---

[1] Work cited, pp. 80, 97, notes.   [2] *Ib.*, p. 92.

critical of all credulities.[1] During these years he must have heard much " definite argument."

Mr. Lecky, sticking to his thesis, after admitting that the " modes of thought " of Montaigne and his disciple Charron persisted, goes on to insist that—

Though the industry of modern antiquaries has exhumed two or three obscure works that were published on the subject, those works never seem to have attracted any serious attention, or to have had any appreciable influence in accelerating the movement. It presents a spectacle, not of argument or of conflict, but of a silent evanescence and decay.

At this stage, the fallacy into which we have seen Mr. Lecky slipping in his preface through sheer laxity of thought and expression has become a positive delusion : so important is it to keep a watch on all our arguments. The process he here speaks of was not and could not be silent : it is absurd so to conceive it. Even if the other books to which he refers were obscure, this would not alter the fact that those of Montaigne and Charron to which he had referred had an immense vogue and influence. To publish such books in those days was a hazardous undertaking : Montaigne profited by royal protection, and Charron ran risks. But though the others were less popular, it is quite gratuitous to say that they " never seem to have attracted any serious attention." The work of Gabriel Naudé, *Apologie pour les grands hommes soupçonnéz de Magie*, won a good deal of serious attention, though, as Mr. Lecky admits, it is " extremely tiresome "—a sufficient reason why it should not be popular, whatever its arguments were. And it " stands to reason," as we say, that the unwritten discussion must have been boundless. What were people to talk about ? what do they ever talk about, if not the matters on which opinions are changing ? Mr. Lecky tells in so many words that " the priests continued to . . . anathematise as infidels all who questioned " the reality of witchcraft, and that " many of the lawyers . . . maintained the belief with equal pertinacity." Against whom ? True, many people who heard the unbelievers

[1] See the *Introduction aux Essais de Montaigne*, by E. Champion, 1900, for a study of the great essayist's development. You will find this book well worth reading if, as I hope will be the case, you are interested in Montaigne.

anathematised might hesitate to speak out ; but out-
spoken doubters there must have been. It is incredible
that a belief once so general and so intense can have
declined without abundant discussion ; and further research would have shown Mr. Lecky further traces of that
in France in the first half of the seventeenth century.

So Mr. Lecky decides that in England the able treatise
of Reginald Scott (1584) " as a matter of fact exercised
no appreciable influence " ; but it is his method, or his
fixed presupposition, that prevents his appreciating influences like Scott's. They cannot reach the mass of a
nation at such a stage of culture as that of Elizabethan
England until they have passed by way of the more
thoughtful few. Now, there are many traces of educated
scepticism in the Elizabethan period, and in the reign
of James. Mr. Lecky goes astray because he looks for
a kind of trace that the conditions did not admit of—
abundant literary allusions. But the very fact that
Reginald Scott's treatise was burned by the order of
King James proves that it was then dangerous to pro-
claim such opinions, though on the other hand such a
treatise could not have been issued if the author were
alone in his views.

How important exact knowledge is to right reasoning
on such matters becomes newly clear when we find Mr.
Lecky pronouncing that Shakspere probably believed
unquestioningly in witchcraft—this on the strength of
the witches in *Macbeth* and the treatment of Joan of
Arc in *Henry VI*. But the experts are now agreed
that Shakspere had no hand whatever in the Joan of
Arc scenes ; and the witches in *Macbeth* merely represent
the natural resort of play-makers in such an age to
any machinery that would attract audiences. There
is no more reason to think that Shakspere believed in
witchcraft than that he believed in the reality of such a
phenomenon as the ghost in *Hamlet*. Those expedients
were common on the stage before his time : he used
them like another, save that, in *Macbeth*, he very clearly
indicates the unreality of the spectre of Banquo seen
by Macbeth, and makes Macbeth's purpose arise independently of the witches. But a playhouse was the last
place where an open attack on a popular superstition
could be thought of. Even to publish a book of such a

drift would have been to incur intense odium, and probably personal danger, all the more because under the  King James and the Puritan clergy ... s becoming more fanatical. Books ... ere lacking, just as books against ... were lacking; but we have clear ... vate talk heresy was often avowed. ... ould such opinions spread if they ... ? Mr. Lecky notes that the anti- ... e otherwise sceptical Glanvil, *Sad-* ... *s*, opens with a picture of the rapid ... in witchcraft. How could that ... it were not much discussed? The ... an extraordinary success." How ... guments were not talked of? ... n the other hand, there were not ... sceptical side, and that those pub- ... tinguished authors; but here again ... he case. At that period, heresy of ... by manuscript than by books: as ... dworth, himself accused of lean- ... red, as to wizards and magicians, ... nt exploders of them can hardly ... of having some hankering towards atheism." Under such circumstances most unbelievers would be unwilling to print, and booksellers to sell, books against the belief in witchcraft; but how could " confident exploders " be recognised if they did not argue?

If you have any remaining doubt on the point, I need but remind you that in the period from 1660 to 1690 there were many declarations by clerical writers to the effect that " unbelief " in general—that is to say, unbelief in Christian dogmas—had become extremely common; yet there were only two recognised unbelieving authors —Herbert and Hobbes—down till 1679; and their arguments do not go very far to assail orthodoxy. It is surely clear, however, that the bitter clerical complaints prove the occurrence of a great deal of private discussion. Yet Mr. Lecky persistently repeats that " the scepticism that was already pervading all classes was steadily and *silently* increasing." [1] A few pages before [2]

[1] *Id.*, p. 121. [2] P. 108.

he had avowed that "there was *manifested* in some classes a strong disposition to regard witch stories as absurd." Such manifestation could not take place without definite argument.

When we come to Mr. Lecky's own comparatively reasonable account [1] of the various influences which promoted scepticism, it becomes still clearer that he has fallen into a confusion of ideas.

The reaction against the austere rigidity of the last Government had produced among the gayer classes a sudden outburst of the most derisive incredulity. From mocking the solemn gait, the nasal twang, and the affected phraseology of the Puritans, they naturally proceeded to ridicule their doctrines ; and having soon discovered in witchcraft abundant materials for their satire, they made disbelief in it one of the tests of fashion. At the same time the higher intellectual influences were tending strongly to produce a similar movement among the learned. Hobbes, who was the most distinguished of living philosophers, had directed all the energies of his scepticism against incorporeal substances, had treated with unsparing ridicule the conceptions of demons and of apparitions, and had created in his disciples a predisposition to regard them as below contempt. A similar predisposition was formed by the philosophy of Bacon, which had then acquired an immense popularity. The Royal Society had been just established ; a passion for natural philosophy much resembling that which preceded the French Revolution had become general ; and the whole force of the English intellect was directed to the study of natural phenomena, and to the discovery of natural laws. In this manner there was formed a general disposition to attribute to every effect a natural cause, which was soon followed by a conviction of the absurdity of explaining phenomena by a supernatural hypothesis, and which rapidly discredited the anecdotes of witches. There does not appear to have been any very careful scrutiny of their details, yet there was a growing indisposition to believe them, as they were discordant with the modes of thought which the experimental philosophy had produced.

Observe here how the fallacious formula of " silent " change, without " definite argument," has led the historian to manipulate his facts. He limits the anti-Puritan reaction to " the gayer classes," and the influence of Hobbes to " the learned." Now, there is plenty of evidence that Hobbes was much read, and still more quoted, among the " gayer classes," who thus had definite argument as well as personal prejudice to influence and guide them. If the philosophy of Bacon had an " immense popularity," the study of *that* cannot

[1] Pp. 109–110.

have been limited to the learned. It is an error, again, and one which damages Mr. Lecky's own thesis, to say that the whole force of the English intellect was directed to natural science : intellects like those of More and Cudworth were admittedly not so directed ; and Mr. Lecky had just been telling us that there was a large new literature in support of the belief in witch-craft. Finally, the opposing movement cannot have avoided " any very careful scrutiny " of the orthodox case. If Glanvil's book was widely read, it must have been widely discussed in detail.

It is for a special reason that I have troubled you with this long analysis of Mr. Lecky's confusion of words and ideas. His thesis that opinions on important issues change " silently " and " without definite argument " is either adopted or independently set up by many people as an excuse for letting intellectual progress take care of itself. Wherever any odium attaches to the main-tenance of new truth, many people who recognise the truth are ready thus to shirk the trouble and possible injury that come from avowing it. In my own case, I have been advised a hundred times by prudent friends not to take part in the criticism of beliefs which they regard as false and foolish. Such beliefs, they argue, will pass away " silently " ; the corrective criticism is " in the air " ; the true doctrine will in time inevitably drive out the false. Such argument, I am satisfied, is not only fallacious but " insincere," in the sense I have given to that term.

Those reasoners, I find, never bethink them to apply their rule to disputes over politics where their views accord with those of the majority, or even to disputes over scientific doctrine where no odium attaches to their own position. Precisely where, on their theory, the truth *might* be left to take care of itself, because the interests of a majority are on its side, they busy them-selves on its behalf ; and where no great interests or prejudices are arrayed against a doctrine of which they approve, they see fit to push it. The " air," in these cases, they regard as a non-conductor : it is only when there are storms in it, so to speak, that they counsel a masterly silence. And Mr. Lecky, as I say, tends to keep them in countenance.

Well, I never found that any truth got into the air and so did its work unless men put it there and kept it there. It is because some men are active and courageous that others can inactively breathe a sound mental air. And I trust that, though that course is not the way to wealth or the widest popularity, you will agree with me in ranking the pioneers, the volunteers on forlorn hopes, higher than the prudent ones, and that you will rather fight for the unpopular truth than for the successful one. In any case, I hope you will recognise the errors of reasoning and of historical statement by which Mr. Lecky has given colour to the counsel of putting your hands in your pockets and your faith in a speechless evolution.

I do not dispute, indeed, that certain changes of opinion take place with relatively little discussion, in virtue of the alterative force of mere social conditions. In a long period of peace, for example, men have been seen to grow less prone to brutal sports and to duelling. When brutal sports decline, there is likely to be a growth of kindness towards animals. But even in these cases, where the initial force is the simple change in the conditions, no considerable change in opinion takes place without discussion. The literature of such discussion, where it gets into print, is apt to pass out of sight precisely because it has carried its point ; but if you will make a careful research, you will find that there was a great deal of literature on duelling and on the kind of treatment of animals before in England the first was discredited and the second made a matter of legislative action.

To make the point clear, let us take one more of Mr. Lecky's applications of his " no-argument " doctrine. Telling of the movement for the abolition of judicial torture, he writes [1] :

In France, probably the first illustrious opponent of torture was Montaigne, the first of the French sceptics ; the cause was soon afterwards taken up by Charron and by Bayle ; it was then adopted by Voltaire, Montesquieu, and the Encyclopædists ; and it finally triumphed when the Church had been shattered by the Revolution. In Spain, torture began to fall into disuse under Charles III, on one of the few occasions when the Government was in direct opposition to the Church. In Italy the great opponent of torture

---

[1] *Id.*, pp. 330–2.

was Beccaria, the friend of Helvétius and of Holbach, and the avowed exponent of the principles of Rousseau. Translated by Morellet, commented on by Voltaire and Diderot, and supported by the whole weight of the French philosophers, the work of Beccaria flew triumphantly over Europe and vastly accelerated the movement that produced it. Under the influence of that movement the Empress of Russia abolished torture in her dominions, and accompanied the abolition by an edict of toleration. Under the same influence, Frederick of Prussia, whose adherence to the philosophical principles was notorious, took the same step, and his example was speedily followed by Duke Leopold of Tuscany.

Here, one would suppose, the effect of " definite argument " was tolerably clear ; read Beccaria, and you will see how ratiocinative he is. But Mr. Lecky bethinks himself that he must not seem to admit the efficacy of definite argument ; and so he gives us this corrective passage :

Nor is there, upon reflection, anything surprising in this. The movement that destroyed torture *was much less an intellectual than an emotional movement*. It represented much less a discovery of the reason than an increased intensity of sympathy. If we asked what positive arguments can be adduced on the subject, it would be difficult to cite any that was not *perfectly familiar to all classes at every period of the middle ages*. That brave criminals sometimes escaped, and that timid persons sometimes falsely declared themselves guilty ; that the guiltless frequently underwent a horrible punishment, and that the moral influence of legal decisions was seriously weakened—these arguments, and such as these, were as much truisms in the eleventh and twelfth centuries as they are at present. Nor was it by such means that the change was effected. Torture was abolished because in the progress of civilisation the sympathies of men became more expansive, their perceptions of the sufferings of others more acute, their judgments more indulgent, their actions more gentle.

I invite you to dissect this passage in its turn with some closeness. Once again, concern for an erroneous formula has led Mr. Lecky to mistake seriously the facts of history. He would have us believe that the treatise of Beccaria, eagerly commented by Voltaire and Diderot, read with deep interest throughout Europe, and acted on by Catherine and Frederick and Leopold, consisted mainly of truisms, "perfectly familiar to all classes at every period of the middle ages." This is sad nonsense. The arguments in question were not truisms, and they were not familiar to any class at any period of the middle ages. Mr. Lecky does not give a scrap of evidence to show that they were. He cites the chapter in Augus-

tine's *City of God* in which the irrationality of torture
is very clearly put; but St. Augustine was the most
intellectual of the Christian Fathers; and his *City of
God*, being an argument against the pagans of his own
day, is not at all likely to have been the most familiar
of his treatises in the middle ages even for churchmen.
Certainly the matter was never so discussed in the
middle ages as to make the arguments against torture
familiar even to lawyers. When Montaigne urged some
of them, late in the sixteenth century, he seems to have
been as suggestive to his readers on that theme as on
witchcraft; and I have noticed only three writers cited
as opposing torture in the century and a half between
Montaigne and Beccaria.

Even in England, where torture had been abandoned
after the Revolution of 1688, there is nothing to show
that the arguments against it had become familiar.
It seems to have been dropped mainly because English
common law, not being consciously based, like the law of
most of the continental nations, on that of Rome, did
not recognise the practice; and its consequent association with the tyrannies of royal prerogative brought it
into political disrepute. Finally, we have Beccaria's
own avowal that he had been led to his philosophical
views only five years before writing his book, the first
influence upon him being that of Montesquieu, and the
second that of Helvétius, who, he says, " aroused my
attention for the first time to the blindness and miseries
of humanity."

It thus appears that sympathy may be aroused and
extended by a ratiocinative appeal. Mr. Lecky's fallacy
takes fresh form in his phrase, " much less an intellectual
than an emotional movement." It is quite true that
some movements are very largely emotional and very
slightly intellectual, in the common senses of those terms:
but on the other hand there can be no great " movement " of an intellectual kind without its emotional side.
Men can be " moved " for a truth, for a reasonable
teaching, as against an unreasonable practice; and Mr.
Lecky's own record shows how essential to the humani-
tarian movement was the reasoned exposition of Beccaria
and his school. I want you to pay special heed to
this—that *every* judgment, every process of reasoning,

has its quantum of emotion : the bare recognition of the correctness of a mathematical demonstration is emotion *in minimis* : one's first sense of the justice and the irrefragability of a great philosophic or scientific doctrine is a marked emotion ; and you will remember Franklin's account of the intense stress of his feeling when he had experimentally proved his hypothesis that the lightning was the same thing as electricity. In such a movement, then, as that for the abolition of judicial torture, where so much human suffering was involved, there must needs be much play of emotion ; but, once more, do not be led by such reasoning as Mr. Lecky's to suppose that humane reforms get somehow made without being argued for. In this very case of Beccaria, as you may learn from the preface to Mr. Farrer's translation of the *Dei delitti e delle pene*, a thoughtful Scotch artist of that day was convinced that the book belonged to " the category of Utopias, of Platonic Republics, and other ideal governments, which display indeed the wit, the humanity, and the goodness of their authors, but which never have had, nor ever will have, any influence on human affairs." No estimate of the kind was ever further wrong. Beccaria's book had an immense, a speedy, and a durable influence, revolutionising to a great extent the criminal procedure of half of civilised Europe, and so gaining ground which has never been lost.

It ought to have been an irksome thought to that artist, if he lived to have it, that such an attitude as his had not only been mistaken, but had perhaps helped to retard a good cause, whose possibilities of success were in the circumstances really great. I trust you will not have such mistakes to look back upon. When you first read these letters you will perhaps be still at the stage of cherishing the ideals natural to schoolboys. I remember how, about the age of fifteen or seventeen, I was deeply concerned about the fighting strength of our country, not at all realising how immensely more important are its social than its military arrangements. I therefore could not appreciate at that age the men and the movements which sought to better the life of peace, with its " wrongs and shames " ; and it needed " intellectual " experience to enable me to develop my sympathies. You, I hope, will not be slower than I was.

I need not again tell you, then, that I am not making light of the forces of emotion when I urge upon you the vigilant use of your reason. The transmutation of emotion is in fact the end of all curative human action ; and the main moral use of reason is to effect such transmutation. But it is in the train of clear thinking only that emotion can be trusted to run. The wrong argument, the wrong belief, has its emotion like the right ; all the cruelties and iniquities of history have proceeded on emotion ; and, as I have been arguing, it is emotion that inspires the majority of bad arguments and blinds men to truth.

In those very matters of the belief in witchcraft and the practice of torture, we have fresh illustrations of the process. Nothing can be clearer than the inconsequence, the irrationality, of judicial torture ; but the demonstration was stolidly resisted by many men trained to dealing with evidence. Why ? Simply because their habits were fixed ; it irked them to hear younger men (it might be) arguing that what they had been doing all their lives was unreasonable ; and they tartly resisted the innovating doctrine ; some proceeding, in the common way of conservatism, to charge all manner of evil bias on the reformers. Beccaria was told that he sympathised with crime.

In the case of the superstition of sorcery, again, we have the signal cases of Glanvil and Bodin, the first a man of markedly critical turn of mind on the side of natural science ; the second one of the most powerful intelligences in the France of his day, and notably rationalistic on the side of religious dogmas. Both set themselves strenuously to maintain the reality of witchcraft when many men of less intellectual grasp and energy were beginning to dispute it. Why did they thus err ? Apparently because they had long been wont to believe unthinkingly in that particular doctrine, because they came late to the facts and arguments which discredit it ; and because their very energy of mind entered into their resentment of the cavils which they may have heard from men of less calibre. Let us say, if we will, that their powers of judgment were unequally developed ; that on some sides their common-sense was feeble ; or that they had not the patience to work out the reasonable induction from the pathological phenomena in which they saw evidence of witchcraft.

In the same fashion, you will remember, some very able and sceptical men of the Renaissance held by astrology, while some men of far less ability rejected it either on " scriptural " grounds or by reason of mere narrowness of mind. But though the astrologers may often have been able thinkers, we may safely infer, I think, that they went wrong because of the *wish* to believe the doctrine that the relations of the stars in space at the moment of our birth determine our careers.

And there is almost no limit, so far as we can gather from history, to the possibility of perverse error of this kind—error of emotional bias, of prejudice—on the part even of critically minded men. Gabriel Naudé, above mentioned, was a good deal of a rationalist for his day, being sanely sceptical about witchcraft where the great Bodin was credulous. Yet his personal and political prejudices led him to condone such an act of ferocious wickedness as the Massacre of St. Bartholomew—a crime denounced and loathed even by many Catholics of the party which committed it.

It may seem to you, when you reflect on all this, that the prospect before poor human nature is rather hopeless ; that error is ubiquitous ; that there is no way of guarding against it. Certainly none of us can wholly escape it : I shall not push you to what Voltaire called " the insane project of being perfectly wise." But be sure that every one of the errors and perversities of which I have spoken was demonstrable at the time of its committal by the processes of consistent reasoning. Every fallacy *is* an inconsistency ; every moral error *is* an insincerity. If you can always remember to revert to the test, " do as you would be done by "—or, more strictly, do *not* as you would *not* be done by—you can never err as did Naudé. And if you never make an affirmation or a negation that is inconsistent with those on which you normally proceed in your beliefs, you will run small risk of being the champion of a doomed delusion. In short, the safeguard against the risks of reasoning is just—more reasoning.

If we can correct the errors of Mr. Lecky, we may surely correct some of our own before they have become

inveterate.   Let us take one more glance at his handling
of the theme above considered—the relative influence
of argument and of other factors on men's opinions.
When he comes to the question of belief in future punishment (hell), he notes rightly enough that theory and
practice reacted on one another : that religious theory
had promoted cruel practice, and that humanised practice in turn tended to humanise religious theory.   Then
he goes on :

> This gradual and silent transformation of the popular concep-
> tions is doubtless chiefly due to the habit of educing moral and
> intellectual truths from our own sense of right, rather than from
> traditional teaching, which has accompanied the decline of dog-
> matic teaching. . . . Descartes, who was the chief reviver of
> moral philosophy, may be regarded as its leading originator.[1]

Here once more there is both assertion and denial of a
silent process, without definite argument.   Mr. Lecky
goes on to ascribe " a real though minor influence " to
Descartes's " purely spiritual conception of the soul,"
which made hell-fire a grotesque irrelevance.   But, a
little farther on,[2] he arrives at the concession that—

> When at last Descartes maintained that thought is the essence
> of the soul . . . he contributed *much* to that frame of mind which
> made men naturally turn with contempt from ghosts, visible
> demons, and purgatorial fires.

I shall not ask you to go with me farther on the track
of this historian's inconsistencies, though you will do
well to look out for them when you read him.   We
have sufficiently made out, I think, the fact that he
phrased and reasoned loosely, frequently forgot what he
had written, and so committed many errors against
which moderate care might have guarded him.   These
are all normal human failings ; and if I am not very
careful, you will doubtless detect some of them in the
course of these letters.   Let such discoveries, above all
things, put you upon avoiding such errors for yourselves.
There is no other profit to be drawn from the study
of error.

[1] *Id.*, p. 336.   [2] P. 343.

LETTER VII

In a previous letter I said I should discuss with you in another the question of " chance." I feel bound to do so because that theme comes up in the course of many lines of reasoning on the serious issues of life, and because it seems to me to set up more confusions of argument than almost any other. Let me warn you then, at the outset, that it is a more difficult problem than it may at first sight seem ; on which score I shall break up my letter into sections.

§ 1

We saw how Professor Minto used the expression : " some other cause than chance." That is, he treated chance as a " cause." Now, I think he would on challenge have admitted that the expression was an error ; because to define " chance " as one of a variety of possible causes of a given phenomenon is to deprive of significance the term " cause " itself, and by consequence to nullify the term " chance."

Let us consider what the word normally means. In such expressions as : " I chanced to meet a friend at the cross-roads " ; " a stray dog chanced to enter the shop " ; " by chance I lit upon this passage in reading " ; or " I chanced to strike my foot against a stone," we mean simply that in such cases the incident is unplanned and unexpected ; or, in other words, that we had not recognised beforehand, or set up by our will, the coincident lines of causation which brought it about. We do not say—unless we speak very thoughtlessly—that it was uncaused : every event, we normally admit, has a cause or causes in previous events. The movements of the stray dog are inferrably the results of causes which we may or may not guess.

The meaning of the term is brought out more precisely when we say over a given phenomenon : this *cannot* have happened by chance, meaning that we are sure it was prearranged by someone's will, or that between two or more of the details of the incident there is a " causal connection." By " causal connection " we mean something that is excluded by the ordinary use of the expression " by chance." If in walking on the street I am nearly struck by a falling slate, I do not infer that it was thrown at me : I surmise either that it had been ill-fastened, and that at length, through a series of minute causes which I cannot trace, it " chanced " to slip loose as I was passing, or that someone working on the roof unintentionally caused it to fall at that moment. If there be a high wind blowing, I readily assign that as the cause. Every step in the whole coincidence is clearly " caused " ; but inasmuch as the forces which moved the slate had no known connection with the motives or forces which brought about my presence at that instant, I call the coincidence a matter of " chance." If, again, it should happen that a man whom I did not know lurched against me in the street, I should reason in the same way, probably surmising that he was tipsy.

But suppose that, in the course of a morning's walk, several men should lurch against me. If they all seemed to be tipsy, and there were many tipsy people about, I should still infer " chance." But if they were the only tipsy or apparently tipsy people I saw, I should probably begin to suspect at the third encounter that they were not tipsy, but were either pickpockets or persons with some design against me. If the annoyance continued, my suspicion would become a certainty. In excluding " chance," then, I assume " purpose." Needless to say, non-purposive coincidences can be very remarkable. A few days before I began this letter I invited a friend, whom I shall call A., to dine with me at my club ; and he accepted. At the hour fixed he did not arrive ; and, " chancing " to meet in the lobby another friend, B., who knew A., I invited him to wait a moment and dine with us. We waited over a quarter of an hour, when B. explained that he could not wait longer. I then went to the dining-room with him,

WILLS'S CIGARETTES

IRD'S-FOOT TREFOIL

iry office a note of my whereabouts. ought to me, at dinner, a telegram at thus : " Disappointed, unable to train ; no other till ten." The tele- town some distance away. Clearly, gone thither on some business, had time ; so B. and I went on with our tes later, however, there was brought someone was waiting for me in the n my descending, I found, after all, addressed to me by name but not by r me : it was unsigned, and not from were only a few other club members , it chanced that one of them was to dinner just as I was, and while e, the other man's friend could not lly, A. had actually arrived imme- elegram ; but by another " chance " he enquiry office had just then been new man had overlooked my note, o wait needlessly.

§ 2

The bearing of such an episode on what is called " the logic of chance " will appear when we proceed to deal with that. The ideas called up by discussion of the term " chance " tend to centre chiefly round what are called games of chance, such as dice-throwing : the word " chance," in fact, comes etymologically from the " fall " of the dice ; and in connection with the phenomena of these games there has arisen a mode of reasoning loosely called " probability-logic." In the throwing of dice we have a play of what is called " pure chance " : that is to say, assuming the dice to be " true," it is quite im- possible to trace or forecast the series of impacts which determine how they shall lie when thrown. From the very fact that we can give no " reason why " certain numbers should turn up, men would begin to grow suspicious if a particular player were to go on many times throwing the same numbers ; and such suspicions, one hears, used at times to lead in dicing-days to the act of breaking the cubes, in order to ascertain whether or not they were " loaded." It is notorious, however, that in all games of chance there occur " runs of luck," independently of any known fraud ; and this very phenomenon, which might be supposed sufficient to convince us of the incalculableness of " chance," has set both gamblers and philosophers on the attempt to find a " law " thereof. The gambler's theories one knows of only by hearsay : they are reputed to be mostly fantastic ; but the thinkers have framed a simple and, at first sight, satisfying theory, to the effect that given results in games of chance occur *in the long run* in the ratio of the " objective possibility." To keep the matter as far as possible on non-mathematical lines, let us take the simple case of pitch-and-toss. The tossed-up coin may come down either heads or tails : these are the only " chances." In the language of the theory of chance " the chances are even " : that is to say, we know no reason why either heads or tails should come up.

But when we say this we simply ascertain and avow our ignorance : we have found and stated nothing whatever as to what *will* happen. Nevertheless the mathematicians, or many of them, cling to the notion that " in the long run " of tossing, heads and tails will come out even. And in this they are supported by what we may call the instinctive expectation we should all have when, say " heads " had come ten times in a series of tosses, the next toss would give tails.

At this point there tends to arise an amusing debate. The late Mr. R. A. Proctor, the astronomer, once had such a discussion in a newspaper with an anonymous antagonist who called himself " An Inveterate Gambler." I have before me some extracts which will show you how they argued. Take, says Mr. Proctor,

" An Inveterate Gambler's " idea that if in fifty tossings of a coin there have been forty heads and but ten tails, the odds are four to one that the next toss will be a tail. Of course this is wrong ; the chances for head and tail are even for that as for every other toss.

He then goes on to say that—

the science of probabilities comes in and explains, what ought to be obvious, that the next tossing is quite independent of all the past ones, and that the betting should be even on " head " and " tail." But Buffon and the other fellows who tried the experiment of tossing a coin many thousand times proved this experimentally. For in all those multitudinous trials it was found that there was not the slightest trace of a tendency towards " head " after (*sic*) runs of " tails," or *vice versa*. There were many sequences of even (*sic*) ten or twelve " heads," yet following these " head " came as often as " tail."

Here, on reflection, you will at once admit that though, if you had not previously considered the subject, you would have been inclined to say that after many " heads " there is *likely* to be " tail," Mr. Proctor is right in saying that " the next tossing is quite independent of all the past ones." In other words, being wholly unable to trace the minute mechanical causation which determines the result, we do not know at all how the toss is determined—we are as ignorant after forty tosses as before. But Mr. Proctor in turn fell into a confusion which I once found surprising, and which I should now describe as the almost inevitable result of an argument proceeding on the belief that there is a " science of probability " in such matters.

In the first place, it is a confusion to say that the alleged " science of probability explains " that the fifty-first toss is independent of the preceding fifty. It is our awakened common-sense that explains that. Mr. Proctor's " science of probability " turns out to be a process of arithmetical calculation ; and there is no arithmetical calculation thus far : we pass the judgment without resort to arithmetic.

In the next place, Mr. Proctor falls into pure absurdity when he says that in the experiments of Buffon and the " other fellows " it was found that there was " not the slightest trace of a tendency towards ' head ' after runs of ' tails,' or *vice versa*." For that matter, a " run of tails " is marked as such by heads before and after : *after* a run of tails there must be a head : if there be no head we are not " after " the run. Mr. Proctor meant that, as a matter of fact, after you have had tails a number of times you *may* go on getting tails. But when he added that " even " (why " even " ?) after sequences of ten or twelve heads, heads *actually did* come as often as tails, he was in effect asserting that in the given experiments runs of thirteen heads were exactly as common as runs of twelve ; and if his argument were coherent he was committed to arguing that runs of fourteen were as common as runs of thirteen, and so on indefinitely. Now, as we are dealing with definite numbers, we know, on principles of mere arithmetic, that this cannot have been so. It cannot even have been true that, up to the figure thirteen, runs of each number occurred with equal frequency. Mr. Proctor has succumbed, as I should put it, to the normal fatality of the theory that there is a " law of chance " : he has been inadvertently saying that there is regularity where in the terms of the problem there is none.

The nature of the fallacy becomes clearer as we follow up the discussion. Mr. Proctor proceeded to explain that in terms of the science of probabilities the chances as it were approximate when we mount into very large numbers. The " gambler," proceeding on his common-sense, avowed that he could not for the life of him see why the mathematical chances should come right in a million tosses any more than in two ; whereupon Mr. Proctor answered :

He is right enough if he imagines the mathematical chances point to absolute equality. In a million tossings, the event actually most probable among many millions of millions of millions of possible events (the actual number is two raised to the power one million, a number containing 301,031 digits, which I would rather not calculate) is that there should be 500,000 heads and 500,000 tails. Yet this chance, though the largest, is largest among a number of chances which are exceedingly minute. The odds are many thousands to one against absolute equality. But they are also many thousands to one against the numbers of heads or tails so disproportioned as 500,500 to 499,500.

In short, there are " many thousands to one against " absolute equality ; but there are more chances in favour of it. That is to say, there is no " science " whatever of the problem in the ordinary sense of that term. The so-called mathematical " science of probability " can predict nothing in such matters as these ; it ends in measuring chance in terms of chance : that is to say, it cannot measure at all. And yet, when all is said, if we were in any way coerced or persuaded to bet on the result of a toss after heads had already occurred ten times running, we might " reasonably " bet on tails, simply because we cannot suppose runs of eleven to be as common as runs of ten unless we also suppose runs of a thousand to be as common as runs of three. And if we so betted, the next toss might nevertheless yield heads ! Such is " chance " : who shall find its " law " ?

§ 3

In view of this standing dilemma, some have argued that " probability " is to be conceived solely in terms of our tendencies to expect certain results. But Dr. John Venn, in his very able treatise, *The Logic of Chance*, argues cogently [1] that this view negates the possibility of a science of real occurrences, and that unless we are to fall back on mere mathematical calculations of abstractly possible relations of numbers—Permutations and Combinations—we must have regard to actual experience, making that our starting-point and point of return. You will agree with him, I think, that mere calculation of the possible combinations of a pack of cards counts for nothing as a guide to action unless it can be shown that actual experiment more or less corroborates the estimate. If the " science " is to consist in pure calculation, we must " go over to the mathematics, and so lose all right of discussion about the things " : rejecting that course, " we take part with the things, and so defy the mathematics."

But what is the result of " taking part with the things " ? What do we or can we know by experiment as to actual averages of such phenomena of " pure chance "—that is, untraceable causation—as the results of tossing coins ? On this head Dr. Venn pronounces so oddly that I feel bound to transcribe the page in full, lest by a paraphrase I should be thought to misrepresent him :

The formula, then, not being demonstrable *a priori* (as might have been concluded), can it be obtained by experience ? To a certain extent it can ; the present experience of mankind in pence and dice seems to show that the smaller successions of throws do really occur in about the proportions assigned by the theory. But how nearly they do so no one can say, for the amount of time and trouble to be expended before we could feel that we have verified the fact, even for small numbers, is very great, *whilst for large numbers it would be simply intolerable*. The experiment of throwing often enough to obtain " heads ten times " has been

[1] Work cited, ch. iv. §§ 12, 13.

actually performed by two or three persons, and the results are given by De Morgan and Mr. Jevons. This, however, being only sufficient on the average to give " heads ten times " a single chance, the evidence is very slight ; it would take a considerable number of such experiments to set the matter at rest.

Any such rule, then, as that which we have just been discussing, which professes to describe what will take place in a long succession of throws, is only conclusively proved by experience within very narrow limits, that is, for small repetitions of the same face ; *within limits less narrow*, indeed, we feel assured that the rule cannot be flagrantly in error, otherwise *the variation would be almost sure to be detected.* From this we feel strongly inclined to infer that the same law will hold throughout. In other words, we are inclined to extend the rule by Induction and Analogy. Still there are so many instances in nature of proposed laws which hold within narrow limits, but get egregiously astray when we attempt to push them to great lengths, that we must give at best but a qualified assent to the truth of the formula.[1]

Here, while coming to a nearly negative conclusion, Dr. Venn lays down the contradictory views that (*a*) we cannot know the average of chances in " large " numbers of instances, because the labour of the experiment would be intolerable ; and (*b*) that nevertheless for large numbers (" within limits less narrow "—a very loose phrase—must mean this, or the argument comes to nothing) a variation in actual practice from the theoretical rule " would be almost sure to be detected " ; and in various passages he seems to avow the belief he has above disclaimed. This confusion would seem to be a survival from an early habit of identifying the numerical theory of chances with the actual course of things.

To that species of miseducation, too, I am inclined to attribute in some degree the attitude of many educated men who, insisting that past chances in no way control future—that after tossing " heads " a hundred times we may just as well have heads as tails—nevertheless insist that in the mathematical " theory of probability " we possess a real science or knowledge. In the terms of their own argument, not only does the theory yield us none but unverifiable propositions : its scientific truth consists in their unverifiability. Professing to give a numerical theory of all chances, they yet exclude all counted or known chances. It is difficult to imagine a more nugatory doctrine ; and probably even academic habit could

[1] *Id.*, ch. iv. § 9, 2nd ed., p. 97.

not keep it in countenance if it were not that useful calculations from actual experience—as in life insurance —are made, as it were, by the same mathematical machinery.

What we arrive at, after discriminating between the different classes of events in regard to which we commonly use the expression " chance," is the conclusion that some kinds of events which singly are " uncertain " or unpredictable as to time and place, but are either certain to occur once in each person's case (as death) or known to occur frequently (as fires and accidents), do in actual fact occur with such a degree of numerical uniformity in time that action can profitably be taken on the basis of such uniformity. Thus the deaths per thousand of the population vary little from year to year, and still less from decade to decade, though a good many of those deaths yearly occur from accidents to strong and healthy people. So with fires : actual experience tells that they occur oftener in certain kinds of business than in others ; hence an adjustment of rates of premium according to " average risk." So with life insurance, and insurance against burglary or accidents. So even with such matters as the number of letters posted annually without addresses : in each order of cases, while it is impossible to predict a given event, we may count on the number of cases being nearly the same in a given period and in similar conditions. Here there is really a " science of probability," albeit one of a very simple order ; and I note that an actuarial expert, after discussing the problem all round, concludes that " the business of insurance has little or nothing to do with the mathematical calculation of chances." [1]

§ 4

These last classes of phenomena have set up fresh confusions of thought in regard to " chance " and " causation." Because, for instance, suicides occur in given populations in nearly the same number every year, varying even from season to season with a good deal of regularity, people are apt to say, " This is *not* chance."

[1] *On Probability and Chance, and their Connection with the Business of Insurance*, by J. B. Sprague, M.A., LL.D., F.R.S.E., &c. (1892).

What seems to be in their minds is the idea, " These things are *caused* " ; and by implication they would seem to hold that " to happen by chance " is to happen without being caused. Now it follows from our foregoing reasonings that both of these notions are fallacies. From the point of view of the general onlooker, accidents and suicides and omissions to address letters *are* cases of " chance," though *all* events are caused ; and in each case of the sort under notice the chain of causation may on enquiry be traceable at will. A suicide is the culmination of a series of causes, all of which may be known to some onlooker ; but to the statistician, and to those who do not know the causes, it is a chance. To the word " chance " we must attach a reasoned meaning : that is all.

Some writers, observing that for many people the word suggests the happening of things causelessly, have confusedly impeached the word instead of the fallacy connected with it. Even so great and so acute a thinker as Hume, by reason of a certain " royal carelessness " about his terms, falls into several confusions on this subject. It may be profitable to you to trace his steps. In his early *Treatise of Human Nature* (1739) he first reasons that " chance is merely the negation of a cause," but proceeds to note more clearly that " 'tis commonly allowed by philosophers that what the vulgar call chance is nothing but a secret and concealed cause." [1] Yet in his essay *Of the Rise and the Progress of the Arts and Sciences* (1742) he writes that " nothing requires greater nicety, in our enquiries concerning human affairs, than to distinguish exactly what is owing to *chance* and what proceeds from causes." What he ought to have said here is : " to distinguish exactly between causal and non-causal coincidences or sequences " ; that is, between cases of causation and cases in which a given event or series coincides with or follows upon another event or series, but is produced by causes apart from that. Finally, in the first of the two *Inquiries* (1748) into which he recast his *Treatise*, he writes, first, that there is " *no such thing as Chance* in the world " [2] ; an extremely

---

[1] Book I, part iii, §§ 11, 12.
[2] *Inquiry Concerning the Human Understanding*, sect. vi, *Of Probability*.

careless way of speaking, which he corrects later by the observation that " Chance, when strictly examined, is a mere negative word, and means not any real power which has anywhere a being in Nature." [1] This brings us to the true statement of the case, which may be worded thus : " ' Chance ' is an expression we use to connote either our ignorance of the causation of a given event or our belief that a given coincidence is not as such causal—that is, has not been planned."

The remark that " there is no such thing as chance " is a sample of verbal confusion which you may do well to examine, because such muddles occur rather often in discussion on difficult questions. As it stands, the phrase is strictly meaningless : it is a mere counter-sense. " Such a thing as chance " means that there *is* chance. Hume meant : " There is no such thing *as some people understand* by chance." Even the phrase, " There is no such thing as a centaur," is but a passable short cut to the proposition, " There is no such thing in Nature as men represent by the figure called a centaur." But Hume's phrase is worse than that ; and it gives a precedent for the now current formula of so-called " Christian Science," that " there is no such thing as Death "—a sense-destroying locution which opens the way for pseudo-reasoning without limit.

I need hardly say, after the foregoing argument, that Hegel falls into a far more serious confusion than Hume's when he affirms that " the world is not abandoned to chance and external contingent causes, but a Providence controls it." [2] Hegel, with all his Pantheism, actually implied that Chance is a force which somehow excludes causation ; for he speaks later of " the empire of chance " and " alien necessity and chance." [3] To such a phrase as " the empire of chance " we can attach only one rational meaning : " the region of untraced or untraceable causes." Hegel then might conceivably mean that a number of the phenomena of the universe belong to that region, but that human affairs do not. This, however, would be both false in fact and inconsistent with his general theorem, for there are intelligible and enig-

---

[1] *Id.*, sect. viii, *Of Liberty and Necessity*, part i, last par.
[2] *Philosophy of History*, Eng. tr., p. 13.
[3] *Id.*, pp. 34, 35.

matic aspects in both non-human and human evolution ; and Hegel is committed to affirming that all alike are the expression of the immanent *or* directing Reason.

His expression then would seem to be a mere stroke of declamation, a figure of rhetoric, a way of being verbally impressive. And his disciples in this connection illustrate afresh for us the difficulty of being sincere in the sense of being philosophically consistent. " Not every trifling occurrence," says one of them, Gans, in the preface to Hegel's posthumous work, " not every phenomenon pertaining rather to the sphere of individual life than to the course of the World-Spirit, is to be ' construed,' as it is called, and robbed of its life and substance by a withering formula." If there be any meaning in words, a " trifling occurrence," to begin with, would be raised to new dignity and significance by being treated as part of the course of the World-Spirit ; and if the World-Spirit means anything it means the organic totality of all human occurrences. If, on the other hand, any phenomena can be said to lose their body and substance by being involved in a withering formula, it may fitly be said that Hegel's formula of the World-Spirit does this for the large masses of history, for the immeasurable processes of human experience which he reduces at times to intellectual abstractions.

Hegel might well complain of " the labour of the notion " : he strained under it ; and some of his confident disciples, as Gans, miscarry badly under the burden. And as I fear that, whether in that way or in another, I am bringing home the sense of the burden in question to you in this letter, I shall here end it, leaving for another the task of grappling with the most important problems in regard to which men use arguments turning on " chance." That task will be the lighter for the relative tediousness of the excursion we have just finished.

LETTER VIII

THE standing confusion set up by the random use of
the word " chance " is seen in full play in the common
argument about the obviousness of design in Nature.
It does not seem likely that the average reasoner will
have got past the plane of that argument in your day,
seeing that he has contentedly energised there now for at
least some centuries. That the order of the universe
cannot have been set up by chance is still, at least, one of
the standing formulas of theism ; and it is ordinarily
employed with the assumption that it involves the conclusion : " therefore, the order of Nature is planned
by an intelligent infinite Person." Let us trace the
usual steps of the argument.

It is common to put first to the non-theist the parable
of the watch found by the traveller in a desert : the
traveller, it is urged, at once realises that he has found
a product of design, somehow brought there, though he
sees no other sign of human passage. In the same way,
says the theist, the universe itself, being a plexus of law
and recognisable order, cannot have come into such
form " by chance " ; it must have had a designing
maker.

Observe that at the very outset the argument destroys
itself. The watch is recognised as a product of design
in contrast with the desert: it cannot have been produced as the scattered rocks of the desert have been.
That is to say, for the theist, the phenomena of the
desert are matters of chance. Yet the very purpose of
the argument is to prove that the whole cosmos, of
which the desert is part, is a product of design : that
there is law and order throughout it. From the play
of intelligent volition in the watch we are analogically to
infer the play of intelligent volition in the cosmos :
yet the argument assumes for its first step that parts of

the cosmos at least show no play of intelligent volition. The modern theist repudiates the ancient theorist's notion of a " fortuitous concourse of atoms " ; yet he assumes for his present argument that the desert is actually a fortuitous concourse of atoms.

Now, taking " chance " in its rational meaning—which is, as we have seen, " uncontrolled or uncontrollable causation of events, inexplicable or unexpected coincidence "—the ancient speculator was really talking reasonably enough. After all the declamation on the subject, it remains a reasonable though not exactly a useful thing to say that " the order of Nature is a matter of Chance " ; for that is only an admission of the plain fact that we have no ultimate knowledge or control of the causation of the order of Nature. We can trace the details or sequences of causation only to a certain extent : beyond that we can but predicate causation as co-extensive with existence, admitting ignorance of the further steps of the sequence.

For the rest, the common argument about the impossibility of a bagful of letter-blocks being shaken out so as to form a rational sentence is a peculiarly gross logical confusion. It *starts* with products of express human design—the letters. Now if we were actually to find a number of sticky balls or lumps in a " state of nature," and shake them violently in a box, so that they finally fell into an agglutinated heap, we should in the ordinary meaning of the term have before us a result of chance—that is, the result of a process of unanalysed causation ; yet that result would be a form of " order," and as such indistinguishable from much of " virgin nature." It may be answered that the adhesiveness of the lumps is itself a mark of design ; but I can carry back the argument to a process of " chance " which should result in the property of adhesiveness, and so on *ad infinitum*. Thus the common argument, so complacently put as conclusive, is so only for people who never think out what they mean by " chance," who beg the question in the act of framing their formula, and who yet virtually reason as if chance meant " absence of causation."

That is the position fallen into by the late Professor Momerie in his book *On Belief in God*, before referred to.

It is there affirmed [1] that the laws or processes of Nature are as they are " either through purpose or by chance." Unless " chance " here means " without causation " the proposition is devoid of significance ; and in that sense no one ever advanced it. Seeking to buttress this nugatory theorem, the Professor writes that

When only eleven planets were known, De Morgan showed that the odds against their moving in one direction round the sun with a slight inclination of the plane of their orbits—*had chance determined the movement*—would have been 20,000,000,000 to 1.

Here we have a dramatic illustration of the confusion wrought in men's thinking by the machinery of the calculus of probabilities. As we have already seen, De Morgan's proposition amounts to nothing ; anything with any number of mere so-called " chances " against it *can* happen, in terms of the theory ; and the phrase " had chance determined the movement " merely stands for failure to attach to the word " chance " any rational meaning. It is somewhat shocking to realise that professional teachers of logic and philosophy can publicly come to such a pass ; but we have already seen, and shall see again, that professed logicians can argue at times as ill as the man in the street. Reduced to significant form, Dr. Momerie's proposition would run : " Either the process of Nature is planned by an intelligence like ours " [he repeatedly insists on such a resemblance], " or its total causation is unknown to us." And this, which he does not in the least mean to say, is, as I have already remarked, perfectly true.

Still, I do not advise you to go about saying " The order of the universe is a result of the play of Chance," for the average person would in all likelihood say *you* were asserting that the order of the universe is uncaused. Besides, the theist would seem to meet you by saying : " It is true we cannot trace the manner of causation beyond a certain point : but we remain certain that the causation is planned. Just as we are sure the watch had a maker, and that it was somehow brought to the desert, though we did not see it made or brought ; just as we should know there was a maker for a new machine such as we had never seen before, and

[1] Ch. iv.

whose working we did not understand, so we know that
there must be a maker for such a stupendous machine
as the universe."

Here, to begin with, the theist is unconsciously re-
stating the contradiction above alluded to. We know
the machine as distinct from the non-machine ; we know
the footprint on the sand as distinct from the non-
human markings on the sand : we know the house or
hut or tent as contrasted with the cave or the plain
or the tree : in other words, the order of Nature is
ostensibly undesigned, design being admittedly the mark
of the human procedure in contrast with the non-human.
But the theist will never submit to the checkmate of the
strict process of his own argument : he falls back on the
conception that from human design we infer in Nature
a design of a different and a higher order. He has
committed, and will persist in committing, the fallacy
of transforming his terms.

Let us then see if we can enlighten him on a higher
plane of argument. Or, say, let me assume that you
are spontaneously impressed by the problem somewhat
as he is—that, in the common phrase, you " cannot
suppose all this frame of things to be without a mind."
This is simply one of the most general forms of what
Ruskin called " the pathetic [he had better have said
the sympathetic] fallacy "—the instinctive tendency to
impute to the aspects of Nature our own emotions—
and it is the very generality of the process in this case
that makes it so hard to detect as such. A very little
thought raises us above the notion that rain tells of
sadness in Nature, that thunder and lightning tell of
wrath, that sunshine stands for good cheer, and so
forth. Once those significances seemed quite obvious to
human beings : to-day all instructed men put them aside
as primitive fancies. But many instructed men still
hold by the *total* sympathetic fallacy—the ascription to
Nature of total purpose, or, in other words, the inference
of a quasi-human " design " for the whole immeasurable
and eternal process.

Now, the philosophic rebuttal of all such inferences
can be put in a proposition belonging to a series which
are of the essence of logic, but which nevertheless much
logical practice seems to leave many men incapable of

realising. That proposition is that *there can be no rational ascription of single mode to the totality of things.* All propositions of mode, all assertions of " manner of happening," in order to be intelligible, must be in terms of contrasted modes. This proposition, again, is of the essence of psychology : all psychology proceeds upon it. Try to frame a proposition of mode, of manner of happening—in other words, of " phenomena "—without assuming contrast with some other mode or phenomenon, and you will see that it is impossible. A term, to be significant, must mark off something else, some other term : a process of happening, to be realised in thought, must be distinguishable from another process of happening : a term of mode, to signify a cogitable process of happening, must imply other processes. Professor Jevons, impressed by this general truth, went so far as to say that even the term " thing " implies the correlative " that which is not a thing "—a proposition which I take to be a philosophic error. The true doctrine, to my thinking, is that " thing " either stands for " everything " or is a non-significant term, like " existence " until it is qualified or quantified. Each of those terms is applicable to every aspect of infinitude. Unfixed, it is like the unapplied vocable " the."

Now, the one proposition of quality, quantity, or *quiddity* that we can rationally make concerning the cogitable universe as a whole is simply—that it is infinite existence ; and that proposition is intelligible in only one way, as the negation of finity, which is the mark of all propositions of mode. To attempt to give to the bare proposition of infinity—a proposition to which we are shut up by the very nature of thought— *any* characteristic of mode, is to commit logical suicide, to produce a meaningless proposition. You will see this readily enough if you try to put any proposition of infinite mode in terms of sense perception : you will never consent to describe the infinite as blue, loud, thin, soft, hot, or sweet. But the reasoning which excludes such propositions leads logically—that is, by the law of consistency—to an exclusion of such propositions as " the universe is purposive," " the infinite is good." A good infinite, in terms of our psychological " first principle," is thinkable only as against a bad infinite :

a designed universe is thinkable only as beside an un-designed one. The abstraction of infinity is intelligible as the negation of every aspect of finity : further than that it is not thinkable at all. Just as it negates limit of extension, it negates mode. And the inveterate habit of talking of a " loving " and " wise " Infinite is simply a persistent refusal to think and speak rationally on such matters.

By the same reasoning, all propositions of " mode of happening " become meaningless when applied to the infinite. The current " idealist " philosophy, for in-stance, tells us that all things are " maintained solely by thought." Now, no matter what perplexities be involved for us in the effort to analyse our ideas of reality, nothing can alter the fact that that is a meaning-less proposition, inasmuch as it affirms one mode of happening for the infinity of things. In order to con-demn it as verbiage, we do not need to confront it with all the other propositions with which, if accepted, it would have to co-exist in our minds. We say, in terms of our first and last principles, that no mode of universal existence, or universal happening, can be thought. You can think of given phenomena as " maintained solely by thought," when you think of other phenomena as not so maintained. Not otherwise can the proposition have any significance. To say that " *all* things, *all* phenomena, are maintained solely by thought," is some-what like saying " all things are soft."

How can it be, perhaps you ask, that such propositions are maintained by instructed men if they be really non-significant ? Can I be right, you may ask, in thus quash-ing as meaningless the formulas not only of theologians but of some philosophers, not committed to theological presuppositions ? Press the question on yourselves, I beg of you. If you can by consistent reasoning refute my arguments, do so. I am doing my best for you : if you can better my best, it will be to you a measurable gain.

Meantime, here is my answer. Such self-contradictory or meaningless propositions as I have instanced seem to me to *have* actually taken rise in the effort to sustain theological presuppositions. The final verbalism, the ultimate meaninglessness, is reached after a number of steps, each one of them plausible, because it deals with a recognised difficulty, but each one none the less fallacious. By a series of minor fallacies or verbalisms, men reach to a sonorous, a clanging verbalism. And it is very hard indeed to discuss metaphysics without verbalism. I am sometimes disposed to think that every metaphysical treatise I know proceeds upon a careless use of words in nearly every page. But it would be vain to attempt to justify such a judgment in these Letters; and it is equally out of the question for me to undertake to present you with my own metaphysic, my own philosophy, under this form. The production of that is a task for long leisure; and I know not whether such leisure will ever be mine. Here it must suffice to work out this one issue of the vogue of meaningless propositions about the Infinite.

The formula, then, that all existence is maintained solely by thought seems to follow upon the formula that " things exist only in our consciousness." Men debate as to whether things exist *in* our consciousness or *outside of* our consciousness; being moved to this debate, historically, by the exigencies of the belief in a controlling Spirit or creative God. Denials of the reality of certain theological conceptions seem to have led to theological denials of the reality of phenomena accepted without question by the anti-theologians; and this verbalist formula, " things exist *only* in our consciousness," is one of the results of that line of movement.

Now, the question whether things exist in or out of our consciousness is, in terms of the foregoing argument, absolutely meaningless if taken as a demand for an account of the *mode* of happening of *all* existence. It is significant solely as a question of *how we shall define " consciousness."* All are agreed that things exist, and that we are conscious of things; and it really does not matter a straw whether we say that all things exist in our consciousness or outside of it. If we affirm " inside," we imply that there *is* an outside—the very thing denied. The debate is one that ought never to have taken place; and it would not have taken place if either side had clearly realised that the question is an attempt to predicate mode of existence of the infinity of things, and that no such predication can be construed in thought. Contrasted modes of occurrence or existence of phenomena are predicable : absolute mode for infinity is a contradiction in terms.

But by ignoring or overlooking this fundamental law of rational statement, and by attaching an illusory significance to the formula " things exist only in our consciousness," men reached the further non-significant formula " all things are *maintained* by thought." From that the next step, equally illicit and inconsistent, is to Totality of Thought maintaining an infinite universe = God maintaining all things. Every one of those propositions is a nullity, a verbal ineptitude, the expression of incapacity for coherent thought on the part of men claiming specially to exhibit such capacity. They are simply saying things that cannot be thought. The entire logical residuum of the argument is the implication that God is a name for Everything.

This is how the case works itself out in that unhappy book of Professor Momerie's, *On Belief in God*. After advancing a series of admittedly indecisive arguments for his thesis, including that about " purpose " and " chance," before mentioned, the Professor proceeds to complete his unconnected series of contentions by one irrelevant to all of them—the theorem now under notice. After setting out with a plea from the alleged universal instinct or surmise of men, he affects to prove his case by a formula which, on his own confession, runs counter to universal instinct—thus stultifying himself for the second time. The universal theistic instinct, he had urged, " is not very likely to turn out altogether delusive " : a sufficiently futile form of words. Now he asserts that " the popular notion of course is, that matter exists apart from consciousness," adding that reflection will show this to be an error. All the while he is merely asserting the truism that we cannot think of matter without matter's being thought of by us. There is " no such thing," he pleads, in the old way, " as an untasted taste." That is to say, there is no *such* thing as no thing. Next we have a formula a little less obviously meaningless, our old acquaintance : " Things exist only in consciousness." Of this proposition the only significant construction is : " We are conscious of things only when we are conscious of them."

Any further implication, such as the Professor is leading his inexpert readers to set up, is a lawless absurdity. Ringing the changes on non-significance, he further affirms that " Things as we know them are the work of thought," which means simply that things are thought by us as we think them ; and again that " There would be *for us* no material world at all except for the activity of *our own minds*." He might have added that if there were no material world there would be no " us." He has in effect merely asserted that if we did not perceive a material world we should not perceive it. And it is from this string of absolutely empty pronouncements that he proceeds to the proposition : " Another Understanding—infinite, though at the same time *in essence* identical with our own—is the source of that orderly system of relations which we know." He might as well claim to have proved that we can digest only in an infinite digestion, or have toothache only in a toothache of the Infinite. The entire argument is a mere swoon of the reasoning faculty, a failure to follow the thread of thought in a small artificial maze of phrases. But that sort of thing passes for philosophy with many men, and many professors.

So strong, indeed, is the spell of a philosophic fashion that we find it yielded to by so independently trained a thinker as John Mill. In his *Examination of Sir William Hamilton's Philosophy*, he sets out on his first enquiry thus :

All language recognises a distinction between myself—the Ego—and a world, either material or spiritual, or both, *external* to me, but of which I can, in some mode and measure, take cognizance. The most fundamental questions in philosophy are those which seek to determine what we are able to know of these *external* objects, and by what evidence we know it.[1]

To me, the proposition in the second sentence seems a mistake : it describes the problems of science rather than the problems of philosophy ; but we may let that pass. What we need to note is that Mill here uses the ordinary or popular language about the " external," and this properly enough, inasmuch as it distinguishes between vitally different orders of experience, as dreams and perceptions. Most of the so-called " idealists "

[1] Fifth ed., p. 6.

would at once object to Mill, as someone has done in a pencilled note on my copy of his book, that " To [say we] perceive something outside ourselves is a contradiction : we perceive only within us : that which we perceive is only a modification of ourselves, therefore within us." This kind of formula has passed current as philosophy for generations ; and yet it is the merest counter sense. He who affirms that we do *not* perceive anything outside ourselves affirms that there *is* an outside, else his proposition is meaningless. Then he alleges that there is an outside but that we do not perceive it. We now come to a mere dispute as to what is to be meant by the term " perceive." The " idealists' " argument implies an absolute confidence as to the presence of the " outside." For that confidence we want a forcible term. Has he any more forcible than " perceive " ? If so, let him put it ; but let him not argue as if the dispute were on a question of fact or existence when it is merely over a question of definition or terminology.

Mill, after the pronouncement above quoted, might be supposed to argue in some such fashion as I have just done. But, proceeding to combat the inconsistent reasoning of Sir William Hamilton, Mill goes on to gainsay himself. Hamilton said that the " primary " qualities of matter [as extension, hardness, etc.,] " are apprehended as they are in bodies ; the secondary [as, colour] as they are in us ; the secundo-primary [i.e. mechanical as distinct from geometrical properties of bodies] as they are in bodies and as they are in us." [1] This I hold, with Mill, to be a tissue of intellectual confusion : no such discrimination of our sense-relations to matter will stand logical analysis. But Mill in the course of his discussion, noting the criticisms of other writers on his, says this [2] :

Mr. Fraser, like myself, believes the Primary Qualities to have no more existence out of our own or other minds than the Secondary Qualities have, *or than our pains and pleasures have.*

Here the term " external," as previously used, is completely negated ; and the new proposition is simply not what Mill previously and normally believed and said.

[1] *Dissertations and Discussions*, pp. 857–8
[2] Ed. cited, p. 41.

He has been led into fantasy by the customary entanglement of terms. The right answer to Hamilton has been missed. The so-called primary and secondary and secundo-primary qualities of matter are alike modes of our total cognition ; and to say that they " have no more existence out of our own or other minds than our pains and pleasures have," I repeat, is to proceed from non-significance to non-sense. The one psychological fact involved is the humble and really unnecessary truism that we cannot think of matter without thinking of it. Matter thought of is matter perceived, remembered, or imagined. Those who say " Matter *cannot exist* unthought-of or unperceived " are merely putting a vicious or unmeaning form on the truism that when we go through the form, say, of imagining a world without people, we are in imagination importing ourselves into that world, and picturing it as seen by eyes. That is simply one of the enveloping conditions of our nature, one of the constituent facts of our existence. We cannot think of stone save as hard, or of fresh grass save as green : in other words, we think the greenness and the hardness. Precisely so ; but the inconsequent corollary, the mere verbalism that we *maintain* the thing as we think it, that it " *cannot exist* save as perceived," says nothing that is thinkable. It is one of those solemn sophisms inventible only by men buttressing false creeds by fallacious systems. This sort of philosophy is of the order of the Nicene Creed : it inherits from the doctrine of the Trinity ; from the *Summa* of Thomas Aquinas and the dialectic of the school-men ; from the ages of pseudo-science which explained Nature in the light of Semitic mythology. But the trick of it, as we see, has become second nature to many men who have transcended those stages of the evolution of theological error. They remain under the spell because they are not good enough reasoners ; because they lose their way in an argument ; because words are too slippery for them ; or because they have been so early reared on sophistries that they have never come to the right and full use of their powers.

This we are driven to say even of Mill, and in respect of yet another error. Oppugning Hamilton's philosophy, which is often acute and penetrating, but chronically subverted by theological presuppositions, he argues on the one hand that " The Infinite," and " The Absolute," as formulated by Hamilton, are " chimerical abstractions," standing for nothing thinkable ; and on the other hand that Hamilton's denial of the thinkableness of infinite " goodness " and so forth is a fallacy. Now, the first criticism is implicit in Hamilton's own statement, for he avows that his Infinite and Absolute are in every way inconceivable, though he theologically claims that they are to be worshipped under " authority." With such teaching we need not now occupy ourselves. But the thesis that the phrase " infinite goodness " is a placing of infinity in a finite category is perfectly valid so far as it goes, and Mill's denial is a sad lapse into fallacy. He goes about to confute Hamilton,[1] first, by the argument that general predicates, such as " good," are all " at least potentially infinite " ; and he actually proceeds to prove this by saying that " good " is a term for all who ever did or will or conceivably can be good, and " this is not a limited number." It is difficult to realise that such an irrelevance can come from a thinker of ability. The question of the number of persons who can be termed good, you will at once see, is wholly beside the case. We might as well say the same thing of the potential applicability of the terms " short," " bilious," " red-haired," " dull." That would not affect the fact that these terms are marks of limitation, which is the conception in hand. Even on his own irrelevant line of thought, he is wrong in saying that the number of applications of the term " good " is " potentially infinite." Here he really does commit the error sometimes charged on him, of confusing the indefinite with the infinite.

He then goes on to admit that the " comprehension " (= incidence) of such a term as " good " is limited. This is the real difficulty, and he proceeds to meet it by arguing that on Hamilton's view—

Infinite goodness cannot be thought as goodness, because that would be to think it finite. Surely there must be some great confusion of ideas in the premises, when this comes out as the conclusion.

[1] *Examination*, ed. cited, p. 104.

All that is conveyed here is a resolute dislike of the challenged conclusion, and I think you will be unable to find anything else in Mill's argument. He takes advantage of Hamilton's error in putting the form " Infinite Space " (= extension) on all fours with " Infinite Goodness " ; but beyond showing that we cannot help concluding in the infinity of extension, he never makes out any case on the true issue. So far as his reasoning goes, it is as valid for saying " infinite shortness " or " infinite redness " as " infinite goodness." Once more, " good," like " blonde," is a term of mode intelligised as in contrast with " not-good " ; and " infinitely good " is either a rhetorical figure or an abuse of language, like " infinitely sweet " or " infinitely round."

Beyond this point Mill's argument becomes an attack on Dean Mansel for saying, in effect, " God is infinitely good, but not in our sense of the term goodness." Mill warmly insists that *this* is a mere vitiation of language ; and here, it seems to me, he is quite right. We might as well suggest a non-human meaning for " heat " or " blue " or " sixpence " as for " goodness." The fitting summary is that the attempt to force theism on the reason must always end in a demoralising departure from veracity of utterance. But Mill, having committed himself to a vindication of the formula " infinite goodness," is left pushing a fallacy against a sophism—a natural result of his setting out with the ostensible assumption that " God " is a clear and valid term, standing for a clear conception. In a note to the second or a later edition of his work,[1] he expressly says that " Conformity to the standard of right has a positive limit, which can only be reached, not surpassed." That is a cancelment of his reasoning about infinite goodness.

It is on this miscarriage of Mill's that Professor Momerie, in a note to one of the later editions of his book on Theism,[2] bases his assertion that Mill " exploded " the idea that there is a contradiction in the expression " Infinite Personality." As you see, there has been no such confutation. Our warranted conclusion is that Professor Momerie, who uses the semi-theist Mill to discredit his fellow-theists Hamilton and Mansel, was simply determined to go on speaking of an Infinite

[1] *Examination*, fifth ed., p. 49.   [2] Rep. 1904, p. 84.

Person as he had been taught to do. "We do not degrade the Almighty," he insists, "by saying that He thinks and knows and wills. If the power behind Nature were destitute of these faculties, it would be infinitely inferior to the poorer type of man." Here we have, in effect, the pretence that those who talk (loosely, to my mind) of a "power behind Nature," think of it by a mere process of eliminating human characteristics and leaving in their concept those of inorganic Nature. Nobody, of course, ever did anything of the kind, and men at the position of Spencer (who taught that his Unknowable must transcend mere Mind) might tell Dr. Momerie that he in turn degraded his deity below birds and fishes, in that he did not conceive of "Him" as able to fly, or to live in water.

You will perhaps now be disposed to agree with me that it is not possible to discourse profitably of "The Infinite" and "The Absolute" except by way of showing the said impossibility. In so far as Professor Bradley, in his very able book on *Appearance and Reality*, aims at something more, he does but illustrate the negative, for his Absolute is just the old "All." Mansel saw that "the Absolute and Infinite can be nothing less than the sum of all reality," [1] and Mr. Bradley shows that Reality includes and is all Appearance. To the same conclusion, unwittingly, comes Professor Momerie when he says that "every existence, divine as well as human, is necessarily conditioned by, or related to, every other." What now becomes of Infinite Personality? We are left facing a collective Everything, of which we cognise a fragment in extension, and a surface in analytic intension.

There is one last device of fantasy of which you will have to take note—that of shifting, as it were, on to the other foot and affirming that Self is the "sole reality." That is the theme of various German philosophies which I shall not here attempt to characterise. It will suffice to show you how the thesis emerges in that of Fichte, as handled by his devoted interpreter Dr. William Smith of Edinburgh—a most worthy gentleman, whose benignant face I well remember. There can have been few kindlier men; and I know few more lawless pro-

[1] *Limits of Religious Thought*, p. 30.

cesses of reasoning than that in which he summarises the Fichtean position in his *Memoir of Fichte*. In Fichte's *Wissenschaftslehre*, he affirms,

for the first time, philosophy becomes, not a theory of knowledge, but knowledge itself; for in it the *apparent* division of the subject thinking from the object thought of is abolished, by penetrating to the *primitive unity* out of which this opposition arises.[1]

On the next page he remarks that—

the *fundamental* character of finite being is thus the opposition of itself (*thesis*) and of something opposed to itself;

but that does not trouble him. Immediately he goes on to assert:

The Ego affirms the Non-Ego, and is affirmed in it; the *two* conceptions are indissoluble, *nay*, they are but *one* conception modified by different attitudes of the mind. But as these attitudes are in every case *voluntarily* assumed by the Ego, it is itself the only *real* existence, and the Non-Ego, as well as the varied aspects attributed to it, are *but* different forms of the activity of the Ego.[2]

Then, after the statement that the Ego's " effort after self-development is the *root* of our practical existence " —the effort being thus prior to the personality—we have this:

This effort is *limited by the Non-Ego*—the creation of the Ego itself *for the purposes of its own moral life*. Hence the practical Ego *must* regard itself as acted upon by *influences from without*, as restrained by *something other than itself*—in one word, as finite. But this limitation, or in other words the Non-Ego, is a *mere* creation of *the Ego*, without *true* life or existence itself, and only assumed as a field for the self-development of the Ego.

And so on, and so on, in an unspeakable beatific see-saw of unruffled self-contradiction. You see how the process is kept up: the good man has settled his formula in advance, and the whole machinery of thought and speech must be violated to yield it as an ostensible logical result. Technically, it all turns on the affirmation in the word " voluntarily," which is explicitly false. This house of cards goes down at a touch from any side: like all idealisms commonly so-called it can give no philosophical solution whatever of the mental phenomena of insanity. If the madman's thoughts are *in*voluntary,

---

[1] *Memoir of Fichte*, 2nd ed., p. 75.   [2] The italics are mine.

we have the result that a million million men, without compact, coincide voluntarily in their concepts of an " external " order, while the involuntarily thinking minority are all at sixes and sevens. And the theorem leaves us to the impressive conclusion that as the Ego is simple perceptionless and sensationless zero when we mentally abstract from it all " influences from without," and as the Non-Ego is a " mere " creation of that zero, without " true " existence, there is no true existence.

As we have seen, the logical answer to all such pseudo-philosophy is that a reduction of all existence to one mode is the mere negation of thought. You will perhaps not feel that you need that canon to justify you in putting aside the Fichtean formula. Our ablest living metaphysician, Mr. Bradley, is fain to reject it, with curious hesitations, on the score that " to make the self absolute is, so far as I see, to postulate in the teeth of facts, facts which go to show that the self's character is gone when it ceases to be relative." [1] That seems ground sufficient ; but perhaps it would have been needless to set it forth in an Appendix if the true canon of relativity had been implicit throughout in Mr. Bradley's system.[2]

Let us now retrace our steps to the problem of Chance, in the light of the principles we have just been considering. We saw at the outset that " design " was realised in thought by the theist only as contrasted with non-design : we now see that this is a law of thought, and that the theist's attribution of design (a term of limitation) to the infinite is a mere vitiation of words, like " soft infinite " and " good infinite." At every point of the so-called design argument the same fatality appears. When we are told to think of the marks of design in the eye, we are implicitly invited to recognise absence of design in the storm, the desert, the cloud. To say " everything is designed " is to distinguish nothing : if every phenomenon is designed, what marks the watch from the wilderness ? Theological people speak of " providential " occurrences, forgetting that on their professed principles *all* occurrences are alike " providential." They are in the grip of a logical dilemma.

---

[1] *Appearance and Reality*, 3rd ed., App., p. 559.
[2] As to this compare Mr. B. Bosanquet's *Knowledge and Reality*, 1885, p. 332.

To give the word significance they must make it contradict their whole theology. Where Hegel stumbled,
how shall they stand ?

In other words—in terms of one of our previous
arguments and definitions—they are either fixedly confused or they are " insincere," in our special sense of the
term, in that they hold by inconsistent propositions
from logically irreconcilable motives. And we are entitled to say of many of them that their aberration is
one of desire, of self-assertion. They will not be content
to admit their nescience, their inability to frame rational
propositions about the infinite. The theologian will not
be content to say, " It *chanced* that I missed taking
a train which was destroyed " : he must needs say,
" God mercifully provided that I should miss that train "
—after he has told us that all of God's provisions are
merciful, and has thus committed himself to the implication that God mercifully killed the other people.
Theology, in sad truth, subsists on men's primary egoism
and on their faculty for false reasoning.

The one element of truth behind all these false pretences of knowledge is simply the truism of the universality of causation. And the false pretences of knowledge
do but obscure that truth. Theology arose in virtue of
the *non*-recognition of universal causation, men going
about to say " God did *this*," because they did not
conceive of him as doing *that*. Thus their very conception of cosmic causation was a delusion when they
first attained to it ; and when some denied their patently
false assertions of supernatural causation they retorted
by charging their gainsayers with denying all cosmic
causation. It may be that the charge was at times
true ; but it is certain that every effort towards a true
conception of causation in terms of universal law or
of simple statement of sequence was met by verbiage
about things not happening " by chance." Thus the
theologian in one breath affirmed and denied universal
causation ; for " chance " really meant in his vocabulary
non-causation, and he had to affirm non-causation as the
condition of some events in order to insist on causation
in others. This we have seen virtually done by Hegel
and his school.

Now that we realise the universality of causation, we

are under no solicitude about affirming the law concerning any phenomenon whatever : our sole concern is to find *what* the causation in a given case is. And it is part of common honesty to admit that all causation is on one level ; that it is all of a piece ; and that as all events and coincidences in non-human Nature which we cannot control or anticipate are for us as much matters of " chance " as such events and coincidences in human affairs, " design " and " volition " are on this view again out of the question. Let me explain. *We* design and will certain things : that is to say, our volitions play a part in the total field of causation. But many things happen to us independently of our volition ; and equally, where we count on and exploit the sequences of Nature, there occur unexpected variations, as in seasons and temperatures, in droughts, floods, earthquakes, blights. If we are to speak of the universe as designed, these are all designed ; but the theist himself does not so regard them in daily life. For the reasoner, who has realised that propositions of mode concerning the infinite totality of things are meaningless, and that design is thinkable only as beside non-design, the assertion is a mere counter-sense. Design is but a mode in the infinite series—a mode appertaining to mind. The infinite transcends design as it transcends mind.

It may occur to you that in assuming the universality of causation I appear to be sinning against the canon I affirm. But it is only a seeming inconsistency ; for causation *cannot* be conceived as contrasted with non-causation : we simply cannot rationally think that any event is not caused. We can but think of it as not caused or controlled by us. That is to say, causation is not finally a modal concept : it is part of the reasoned concept of sheer existence ; whereas design is a modal concept, because we can and do conceive of events as undesigned, and the very assertor of universal design habitually does so, and implicitly confesses it.

And now we come to the twofold crowning anomaly of men's debates on the order of Nature. The very theologian who insists that the whole universe is designed, openly turns round at a certain point and insists that it absolutely lies with us to determine our acts ; that our volition is " free " ; and that we are therefore responsible

to the universal designer for what we do. In the terms
of the proposition, " he " designed the universe of things
and events, which includes us and our deeds ; yet after
all " we " are the masters of our volition, in the sense
that we do wrong when we could have done right, and
vice versa. Thus does inconsistency go from bad to
worse. By a quite intelligible sequence, the proposition
of " Infinite Design," which is only formally rational, is
followed up by a proposition which formally annihilates
it : " We are uncontrolled in the exercise of our will,"
that is, " our acts are not part of Infinite Design." I
shall deal with that problem in another letter. Meantime, take note of the intellectual insincerity of the
school which affirms this proposition after that other—
the non-determinateness of men's wills in the same breath
with the foreordination of all things.

And that contradiction is paired with yet another.
The same assertor of the designedness of the entire order
of Nature practises prayer to the designer, and affirms
its reasonableness. It is important to keep those facts
present to your mind when you are discussing the vital
problems of belief about the totality of things. You
will read what are ostensibly most earnest asseverations,
confident arguments, calm claims to have set forth irre-
futable doctrines ; and you may find it hard to with-
stand such a show of sincerity. But it is all the while
the literal fact that some of those ostensibly convinced
reasoners are affirming contradictions as gross, shib-
boleths as meaningless, as words can be made to frame.
And while I insist that such persistent inconsistency
connotes insincerity, I must proceed to explain the per-
sistence, the insincerity, in terms not merely of egoism,
of partisanship for one's formed or inherited opinions
and dogmas, but of the difficulties of coherent analytic
reasoning on the deeper problems of life, the imperfect
structure of the thinking faculty, and the still more
faulty cast of the tools of reasoning—to wit, words.
From among many testimonies on that head, let me cite
to you that of an able reasoner whom I shall further discuss with you later, the Reverend Jonathan Edwards, of
famous theological memory. It is over the problem
which wrecks his otherwise well-sustained argument that
he is fain to make this confession :

Language is indeed very deficient, in respect of terms to express precise truth concerning our own minds, and their faculties and operations. Words were first formed to express external things ; and those that are applied to express things internal and spiritual are almost all borrowed, and used in a sort of figurative sense. Whence they are, most of them, attended with a great deal of ambiguity and unfixedness in their signification.[1]

Language is in short an instrument still stamped with the ineptitudes of primeval thought, still crooked from the fallacious bents of dawning intelligence. This, which we should regard as the greatest of all the arts if it were not the only one acquired by all save the malformed, is the least improvable of them all. The other arts can rise on stepping-stones of discarded and disregarded models ; but this had always to carry in itself the perversities set up by outgrown ideals. In painting and sculpture, even in the art-forms in which language is the material, we can try new methods, discarding a poetic as we do a pictorial convention ; but the primary art of speech is only by pitifully minute degrees capable of transformation. In some aspects, indeed, the evolution is considerable : in the specially artistic aspect of expression it is marked and relatively rapid ; but as regards the improvement of the labour of sheer thinking, it is slow and difficult. For mental analysis, so to speak, we must still use the stone axe, the knife of flint : witness my very metaphors. We cannot shape a new speech by taking thought : developed reason is bound to the use of the implements forged by the blundering barbarian.

You will find it, by the way, a useful discipline in thinking to scan carefully anything you may write, for laxities of expression. A habit of correcting these is at least a lead to accuracy of argument. All writers fall into them now and then. George Bentham, in his *Outline of a New System of Logic* (1827), pointed out a startling instance in Archbishop Whately's phrase charging certain cultivators of Natural Philosophy with " *overlooking* the *boundless* field that was before them *within* the legitimate *limits* of the science." [2] Yet that absurd " bull " was never corrected by its author, for it stands in my copy of his book, published in 1850. In

[1] *Inquiry into the Freedom of the Will*, ed. 1790, p. 324, part iv, sec. vii.
[2] Whately's *Logic*, introd.

Mill you may find many less flagrant lapses, for example, such a tautology as "final termination."[1] Some exquisite writers, it is true, are very incorrect thinkers on abstract themes; but I fancy that watchfulness over phrasing promotes as it is promoted by accurate thinking; and indeed the correct or finished writer is so by reason of thinking closely so far as the expression of his own meaning goes.

And as with speech, so it is with conduct. Only in a few may the life of thought develop in even partial independence of the huge pressures of habit and inheritance: error lies about us from our infancy, and we mostly grow up with opinions as we grow up with appetites and tastes. Thus the struggle of opinions takes on the ways of the struggle for life, so headstrong, so little moralised. The struggle, in short, is all one; and it is all Nature. Men's inconsistency in simple matters of conduct, of personal relation, is in the mass so monstrous, so shocking, that merely to reprobate it is in a manner to evade the confession that moral perversity is a part of the order of things. And it is wholesome to face and confess that fact chronically; for only thereby, unless we be singularly endowed with love, can we hope to keep in charity with our opponents —a thing the more desirable because, if we can infer the future from the past, the theologians among them will certainly not keep in charity with us.

My meaning will become more clear when I discuss with you the problem of Freewill, which has been by some uncharitably called the *pons asinorum* of moral philosophy. That definition, alas, is much too exclusive in the present state of civilisation. Our bridge is narrow, and really not easy to cross; and I should prefer to call it in all good faith the *pons theologorum*, the bridge at which the theologian (now) balks. To cross it, you need a cool and a clear head, and a quite frank curiosity. Take a rest, then, before you approach it.

[1] *Examination of Sir William Hamilton's Philosophy*, pref. to 3rd ed.

LETTER IX

THE moment the issue of " Free-Will " is posited, we are on the verge of a snare constituted by the crudity of the terms with which men first had to work. Let us watch how they have been wont to stumble into it in the past.

Ages ago, no one can say when first, men were led to brood on the spectacle of human conduct, the play of passion, the as-it-were flagrant fatality of the course of some ; the dooms of strange misfortune, signal prosperity ; the wide diversities of character which seemed to constitute or determine fate ; and the no less wide diversities of fate which seemed to determine character. Out of the common brooding and guessing arose that dim notion of Fate ; of dooms laid by capricious or conflicting Gods, whose will men might not resist. And among those who doubted the existence of such Gods— a type of intellectual variation that tends to arise in every stage of human evolution, but is hard put to it to prosper in any, thus far—there rose the guess that the inferred compulsion lay in the far-off but strangely enduring stars, whose courses, with cyclic variations, were seen to last from age to age of transitory humanity. Sometimes the Godites accepted the astrological hypothesis, being undisturbed by a fallacy the more ; sometimes they resented it as doing dishonour to the Gods. And when, in special conditions, there rose a special passion for what was held to be righteousness, the men most swayed by it were apt to insist that the Gods or God sought only such righteousness, and that men's misdeeds came of their own depravity, or else of their subservience to evil spirits—Gods discredited for the time being.

Such an attitude was proper to narrow and strenuous minds, especially to the worshippers of a single God, much feared in their world; but in communities of an intellectually freer or more cosmopolitan cast the compulsions of character and circumstance were more justly considered; and with the mixing of races went an interchange of theories, most civilised peoples harbouring both. Thus the later Jews, drawing on the cosmopolitan thought of Babylon, accepted the dogma of an original depravity, transmitted fatally from the first man to his descendants; yet all the while held men as punishable by their Maker for their sinfulness. Similarly the historic Greeks held by the thought of a Fate either imposed by some divine volition, swaying men to their own undoing, or enveloping and determining the very Gods themselves, yet never thought of adjusting to that thought their customary law. Thus was the riddle passed on through the generations, with chronic debate, the stress of it sometimes turning on the justice of the Gods, sometimes on the guilt of men.

In the specialised cults which turned to fresh account the primordial superstitions of sacrifice and atonement, both sides of the contradiction naturally persisted. The worshipper was declared to be under the curse of a general if not of a particular guilt; and the special sacrifice or ceremony took that guilt away: hence faith in the sacrifice was for the priest the first and last stipulation, the indispensable thing, and as such a virtue in itself. But alike in the consciousness of priest and of worshipper, " natural " or quasi-critical ethic tended also to hold its ground; and there struggled forth in the Christian world in particular a confused compromise, in terms of which all men were prone to sin, and needed grace from on high even to repent, yet were reprehensible for not repenting, for not having grace. But at every conscious adjustment the crux took fresh form : you would get grace if you prayed for it; yet since many were obdurate, you clearly needed grace to pray. The anomaly had a firm hold further in respect of most men's consciousness of their own moral variability, which the antithesis seemed vaguely to explain, yet did not solve. And as surely as the demoralising bias of ritual and the sacrificial principle reduced morals to mummery, the rebelling conscience of the more thoughtful, with its recurring variations towards common-sense and manliness, insisted that virtue and vice lay in the will, and were to be measured by right and wrong action. On the other hand, the challenged priesthood, menaced on their central standing ground, reverted in more or less good faith to the philosophic defence that if God ruled he must rule men's wills ; and the pagan demonstration of the cosmic reign of Necessity was employed to confute Christian heretics who sought to throw men back on their own moral judgment and initiative. I do not say that this sketch covers all the ground of the evolution in question ; but it will serve broadly to indicate how the form and fortunes of a particular philosophic problem are determined by a long chain of historic circumstances.

For the modern European world the problem was set up on high, as it were, through the sect-strifes following on the Protestant Reformation. What at first sight seems odd, the Protestant Churches, professedly revolting at the immorality of the Papal, did not set up as against the Catholic doctrine of sin and penance and confession and absolution a doctrine of individual responsibility and retribution such as would make morality a matter of reciprocal human duty. On the contrary they stressed heavily the old Augustinian doctrine of predestination and arbitrary divine grace, which in the fifth century had triumphed over the heresy of Pelagius, who stood for the moral freedom of men. Despite that triumph a confused compromise followed, and four centuries later the predestinarian doctrine of Augustine was condemned as a heresy in the person of the monk Gottschalk—so signally do heresy and orthodoxy change places under changed circumstances. It would seem that the authority of Augustine was able to carry the dogma of predestination in his day because in that time of political ruin the fatality of things had come very deeply home to the southern clergy, part as they were of the falling fabric of Rome ; while the northern Pelagius, nourished on Greek lore, expressed the surviving spirit of human energy. When in the ninth century Gottschalk, a brooding monk, insisted vehemently on the high Augustinian doctrine, he was angrily resisted both by the scholarly Bishop of Mayence, Rabanus Maurus, and by the Gallic Archbishop Hincmar ; and at the same time the temper of self-assertion, natural to a tempestuous barbarian world, found again in John the Scot (i.e. the Irishman) a mind, trained like that of Pelagius in Greek thought, to give it nobler expression. In so far, however, as the question was ecclesiastically decided against Gottschalk, who was flogged and imprisoned, it was judged partly on economic grounds (Churchmen feeling that Gottschalk's doctrine struck at their power as dispensers of saving sacraments), and partly on grounds of regional jealousy. Thus the problem was never philosophically or even officially solved, inasmuch as John's very remarkable rationalistic pantheism is not at this point clarified ; and his startling rationalism heightened the reaction in Gottschalk's favour, with the result that Hincmar in turn was condemned as a heretic in two councils, and the Church in general receded towards the anti-Pelagian teaching of Augustine.

In the sixteenth century the lines of opinion were again determined largely by political conditions, for though Luther's early study of Augustine had much to do with his creed, his opposition to indulgences and his relation to the Church of Rome counted for more. Early reformers like Pelagius had sought to upset ceremonialism by denying predestination : Luther and Calvin, with the same aim, affirmed it. The reason was that Protestantism, if it was to fight Romanism with any success, had to stress at once the scriptural side of Christianity and the belief in the principle of atonement, insisting only that the atonement operated not through the functioning of a special priesthood, but through absolute divine fiat laid on the whole nature of things. Thus divine foreordination became a Protestant tenet ; and there ensued the singular spectacle of another general reversion in the Church of Rome to an ancient heresy of common-sense, in contravention of the teaching of its first great theologian, Augustine. Either way, the object was the same, to establish the special claims of the historic Church as against dissidents from its practice.

On both sides the moral confusion was boundless, essentially because both sides started from premises which could not be reconciled with rational moral practice—the premises of an omnipotent and all-good Creator who foreordained human sin while reprobating

such sin, and who satisfied his own sense of justice by
sacrificing his son as an atonement for the sin thus at
once foreordained and condemned.   On this ground, the
most powerful intelligences fought without the slightest
approach to solution, merely revolving in opposite circles.
Start from their premises and you will see the fatality.
If the posited God be administrative and omnipotent,
he must have foreordained all things : if he willed that
men should sin, he can have no rationally intelligible
right to condemn or punish them.   Over this dilemma
many disputants took up opposite positions which equally
annihilated rational morality : one side insisting that the
potter was free to do what he would with the clay,
which could not without blasphemy challenge him ; the
other arguing that what God willed could not be wrong,
and that the provision of the atonement was made
expressly to balance all human acts, which were thus
all alike permissible.   But the natural moral-sense or
common-sense in turn, though still bound by theology,
revolted from both extremes : the more orderly pre-
destinationists on their side insisted in the same breath
that God foreordained sin and repentance, salvation and
damnation, at his free will, and that all the same he was
perfectly righteous and a hater of sin ; while on the
other side there arose new Pelagians, notably the fol-
lowers of Arminius, who more or less clearly argued that
sin and salvation were not foreordained, and that all
men were free to seek and win salvation, but that none-
theless God was omnipotent and foreknew all things.

From these opposing circles you will see there is no
rational escape while the premises stand.   You have
your line A B, the dogma of creation by a Good Infinite
One (a twofold contradiction in terms, since Infinity is
that which cannot be added to and cannot be thought
as having finite mode), and you simply describe your
circle either from the point A or from the point B,
neither argument ever absorbing or excluding the other.
Start from God's creative omnipotence and you have
the thesis of Calvin : start from God's Infinite Goodness
and you have that of Arminius.   Both points of the
premiss are vain figments ; yet fixed and sacred premisses they remained.   And they so remained for this
among other reasons, that, fatally false as they were,

they distortedly represented for men the two fundamental facts of moral science : the absolute continuity
of causation in human as in non-human phenomena,
and the necessary reference of all moral judgment to
individual character.

What, then, is the rational solution ? Shall we affirm
either with the Arminians that " man's will is free," or
with Luther that " man's will is slave " ? Or, coming to
the modern aspect of the struggle—for it goes on to-day
as between theists and naturalists—shall we say with
the Determinists, " man's will is determined," or with
the theologians, who as a body have performed one
more complete change of front, " man's will is left free
by God " ? At first sight there is something bewilder-
ing in this perpetual changing of sides ; heterodoxy and
orthodoxy alternately ranging on this side and that, as
in a dance. It is worth while, before we come logically
to close quarters with the problem, to realise why those
repeated transformations have latterly come about.

Broadly speaking, the old Pelagians, as aforesaid,
denied predestination by way of maintaining rational
moral motives against a dogma which was destroying
them ; and the Church held by predestination because
that doctrine on the whole best consisted at the time
with its hold over men's minds. Later, in a much
divided world of feudalism, that very doctrine was seen
to lend itself to anti-priestly heresy, and was condemned ;
till the rationalism of some of its opponents drove orthodoxy back towards the predestinarian position. The
first Protestants, in turn, held by predestination because,
when once men had on other grounds broken away from
Rome, that doctrine was as good for them as for it, and
was as it were a bulwark of conviction against Papal pre-
tensions. Rome then returned to quasi-common-sense
because that could be used to discredit Protestantism,
with its licentious sects ; and Protestantism, in turn,
prudently alternated its theoretic predestinationism with
a popular asseveration of all men's freedom to come to
grace.

Newer rationalism, in turn, rebelling against the doctrine of eternal torment, adhered to by Catholic and
Protestant alike, insisted on the one hand on the
enormity of eternal punishment for foreordained sin,

and on the other hand pressed against arbitrary theology the truth that *belief* is not a matter of volition, the will being absolutely determined by motives conditioned by structure of the mind. In the very different hands of Spinoza and Collins this line of thought led to powerful philosophic demonstrations, which struck at the very bases of the Christian creed of salvation by faith. And as these demonstrations brought out constantly the principle that all events and acts, including all volitions, are determined by antecedents, it was clearly the cue for Christian theologians to retort that such Necessitarianism (so it was called) made an end of all human responsibility; that it would thus reduce society to anarchy; that morality depended on the fact of the freedom of the will; and that *therefore* God had left men's wills free. All the while their own theology had twice over, in principle, destroyed the basis of rational morals—by its doctrine of predestination by a Good Infinite and by its doctrine of atonement and salvation by faith. But these circumstances, of course, were not put side by side with the new formula of free will. It was the general cue of theology to appeal to the sanctions of quasi-common-sense morals, and this was duly done.

Now let us come to the logic of the problem. It is philosophically to be solved at once on the fundamental logico-psychological principle indicated in my last letter —that of the thesis that propositions of single mode cannot rationally be made of the infinity of things. On the same grounds with that proposition stands this, *that terms of relative mode cannot rationally be used absolutely of an endless series absolutely considered*—or, in other words, that terms of relativity become non-significant when employed to exclude relativity of mode in an infinite series which is itself not thought of as one of two or more correlative modes. Let me explain in detail. When we think of, say, crows, we mentally define them against other birds; and the statement " all crows are black " is perfectly significant. But when we think of volitions *as such*, we can define them against no correlative; they constitute for us an absolute or infinite series; being coextensive with thought, they belong to no wider species. Any ascription of mode to them, then, is intelligible only as connoting other modes; as

" weak," implying " strong." That is to say, we can never describe them *all* by a relative term—always excepting the terms of causation, as already explained. And since I can say " weak volition," only because I can recognise also " strong volition," so I can affirm " free volition " only if I recognise also " unfree volition." To say " all are free " is like saying " all are weak." The moral world is the world of moral judgments, choices, the world of volitions: if, then, we apply a term of moral mode to *all* volitions (an infinite series, having no defining contrast,[1] since non-moral phenomena are wholly out of the question) we reduce it to absolute non-significance. But, equally, " unfree " cannot be predicated of the totality of volitions: the formula " the will is not free " = " all volitions are non-free " is just as meaningless as the other. Common-sense has here come to grief by reason of the primitively unfit tools with which it worked. " Free " is a term significant solely as contrasted with " unfree "; it arises as a description of a state or mode of being and doing, and is applicable only to certain states of being and doing as contrasted with different states. Now, it is not suggested on either side of the free-will dispute that some volitions are free and others not free: that notion is excluded by all as unthinkable; therefore it is at once logically clear that the terms have no rational bearing on volitions at all.

One philosopher of good standing, Dr. Shadworth Hodgson, has indeed endeavoured to reconcile indeterminists to the determinist view by showing that, given determinism, there is a " real free-will " in respect of certain acts as compared with others; that is to say, there is *not* free-will in such a case as an intensely thirsty man's resolve to drink the first liquor he sees, that being " action determined by a single unresisted motive." Processes of *deliberate* choice, on the contrary, he describes as " really free " volitions. But unless we are to suppose on the thirsty man's part a mere reflex action (" consensual reflex action " is a phrase apparently meant to convey such a view), in which case there is no " choice " at all, this discrimination is only one more fallacy, for the difference between the thirsty man's

[1] As it is put by Spinoza at the beginning of his *Ethica*: " *At corpus non terminatur cogitatione, nec cogitatio corpore.*"

choice and that of the less thirsty man is only one of
degree of intensity of motive, his choice being "*any*
drinkable liquor *rather than* more thirst." Unless he
be insane, however, he will *not* drink boiling water, or a
known deadly poison. The problem, then, really remains as it was. If there be anything in the argument
before us, it would be equally valid as regards the case
of a man with an overwhelming bias to drink alcohol to
excess when he might drink water : of his case, too, it
would have to be said that it showed " no trace of free-
will." But this is not suggested, or apparently seen,
by Dr. Hodgson. He has erred in the usual way in
stating the problem, for he seeks to confute those who,
he says, " deny the freedom of volition," and so would
" rob the words *duty, conscience, right*, and *wrong* of all
distinctive meaning." The logical course would be, as
above contended, to point out that denial of " freedom of
volition " is equally with assertion of it a spurious predication, a meaningless proposition. If any determinists,
so-called, talk of " necessity " and " compulsion " in
the process of volition, they are morally reverting to
the theological fallacy (which we shall consider later),
and logically reverting to the fallacy of predicating one
term of a relation concerning an absolute series to the
exclusion of the other ; for " necessity " and " compulsion " are only synonyms for the negation of freedom.[1] But Dr. Hodgson implicitly commits the same
fallacy. For lack of a true logical analysis, in short,
a whole series of recent thinkers have, as we shall see
further, added fresh confusion to a problem which they
should have formally cancelled as illicit.

What men are confusedly pointing at when they speak
of " free " or " non-free " volition is the pseudo-problem
whether volitions are caused or uncaused. But " non-
free " is not equivalent with " caused," and " caused "
is not the antithesis of " free " : they conceptually

---

[1] J. S. Mill (*Logic*, B. vi, c. ii, §§ 2, 3) rightly condemns the use
of the word necessity in this connection, but does not show, as
he ought, how it is theoretically or logically wrong, and in his
anxiety to oppose the Owenites he himself falls into confusions.
The former objection applies also to the otherwise decisive argument of T. H. Green (*Prolegomena to Ethics*, B. ii, c. i, §§ 106–10) ;
but he avoids Mill's confusion, though the editorial synopsis of
§ 108 obscures its argument in Mill's sense.

quadrate or compare in no way whatever, any more than " black " and " long." Causation, as I said before, is not finally a modal or differentiating conception at all : it abstracts itself in thought as an element in every rational conception of existence or happening ; and there is no psychic or ideal contrast to it, since non-causation is merely a word to which on reflection no concept whatever can logically be attached. " Un-causedly " can be made to do rational duty only as a bad synonym for " inexplicably " or " unintelligibly " caused, as when we talk of a " causeless caprice " or " causeless anger."

It may occur to you here that I am " begging the question " as regards volitions—taking for granted the thing in dispute. Rather I am applying a logical law which quashes the form of the dispute, even as it would dispose of a dispute as to whether infinite length is hard or soft.[1] But as it happens that even men who ostensibly recognise the co-extent of causation with exist-ence, the aspect of causation in all happening (our tools here, you see, are still sadly clumsy !), yet stumble over the figment of uncaused volitions, I will now go with you over the ground *a posteriori* in order to bring home to you the reality of causation in the world of volition as it does come home to us when we begin handling the problem from within.

We cannot do better than take it up in company with Jonathan Edwards, who approached the problem from within, recognising indeed the logical meaninglessness of the ordinary formulation,[2] but reasoning nevertheless from point to point of the concrete case with a calm coherence of power which marks him a born thinker. He might have found in Spinoza and in Hobbes the

---

[1] J. S. Mill argues, as against Professor Bain (*System of Logic*, 1-vol. ed., p. 26, *note*) that " we can certainly predicate of a sound, or a smell, that it is not white." We certainly *can* utter verbiage ; but we can also refuse to debate about it ; and meaningless pro-positions should not rank as predications.

[2] E.g., when he remarks that " in propriety of speech neither liberty nor its contrary can properly be ascribed to any being or thing but *that which has* . . . will. . . . For the *will itself* is not an agent that *has a will* ; the power of choosing itself has not a power of choosing." (Pt. I, § v.) This was previously pointed out by Strutt and by Locke.

finished form of the argument he was compassing ; but as a devout Christian he had abstained from reading Hobbes and Spinoza ; and he forced his way through the argument in the character of a Calvinist determined to clear up the issue as between himself and the Arminians. His demonstration is broadly in this wise.

Criticising Locke, he notes that " A man never, in any instance, wills anything contrary to his desires, or desires anything contrary to his will " ; all alleged cases of that kind being so merely through miscarriage of the terms. The will, then, is determined or set to work by something, and unless it is " a cause that acts and produces effects upon itself " it is determined by motives : that is to say, " the will always is as the greatest apparent good is," or " the will is always determined by the strongest motive." But it is obvious that different men are very differently affected by the same appeal, that a given motive acts in them in very different degrees, and that it may act in the same man with different force at different times. Some men, in fact, are either always or occasionally " morally unable " to respond to a given moral appeal. This may be a matter either of instruction or of natural bias. A good man, broadly speaking, is one whose bias is good. In other words, his will is predisposed to good actions, so that he does without struggle of inclinations what another does only after struggle, or, for lack of sufficiently strong good inclination, does not do at all.

But here arises a crux for both the naturalist and the theist. If I happen to have strong inclinations to evil and yet conquer them, am I more or less " virtuous " than one whose inclinations are wholly or almost wholly good ? The question is often answered by both theologians and non-theologians with an award of special merit to the character which triumphs over its evil inclinations. Theology used almost normally to make virtue consist in self-denial ; so that the man with the most complete inclination to good must presumptively be good with less " virtue " than one who had strongly conflicting inclinations. But common-sense, though apt to endorse the view that the latter type deserves special praise, is apt also to be staggered by the consequence that a man gets credit for special virtue on the strength of the bad elements in his nature ; and both the latter-day theologian and the early rationalist have been moved to " hedge " over the problem.

Then there is the further theological crux : If the bad man is so by reason of an over-plus of bad inclinations which are *innate*, how can he be deserving of punishment as compared with the good man, who, so to speak, could not go wrong ? The first instinct of both the theologian and the natural moralist, on seeing the point, is to fall back, however inconsistently, on the notion that all men start alike, and that it is by " their own doing," so to speak, that they come to have an overwhelming bias towards evil. But this position, in which many theologians stolidly persist, is a mere evasion of the problem ; for we are left asking : If all start alike, why do some *begin* to diverge to the wrong side ? Why does anyone will towards evil ? On this view, *C'est le premier pas qui coûte.* If A from infancy leans to the right side and B from infancy leans to the wrong, what is the primary cause ? Observe that if you say there is *no* predisposing cause (and many theologians in effect say this) you have at once denied the principle of causation in the universe and quashed the theological theorem of design, as well as that of " original sin." Theologically speaking, God on this view did not design anything whatever in regard to men's wills : non-theologically speaking, causation is given up, and reasoning ceases.

All this Edwards saw with perfect clearness ; and accordingly he is firm in his Calvinistic doctrine that " God " did foreordain how men should will and act. It was for him, as a devout Christian, the only way of conceiving causation, the only way of being rational and consistent in his thought. But in virtue of his consistent theism he inevitably proceeds to propositions which utterly repel the civilised moral sense ; and, seeking to salve his conscience at a critical point, he no less inevitably destroys his previous argument. Up to a certain point he proceeds securely, save that he needlessly abandons his logical foothold as to the meaning of " liberty." Inasmuch as liberty means the power to do as one pleases, he said, one must " please " or desire something in order to experience liberty. This

bias, then, is clearly not a negation of liberty : it is
the condition of the realisation of liberty ; and it was
logically unnecessary, as regards the human problem,
to argue as Edwards does after Locke, that no one can
conceivably desire to have been without predisposition.
That would be " to desire to have no desires "—a contradiction in terms.

As regards virtue and vice, again, Edwards sees and
shows that both consist in bias or predisposition,[1] and
that it is vain to say a man is not wicked or reprehensible because his evil bias is innate, since it is just
markedly evil bias that constitutes wickedness or repre-
hensibility.   But as soon as he comes to close quarters
with his theology he begins to do alternate violence
to good feeling and to rectitude, to moral instinct and
to consistent reasoning.   Much of his argument is given
to purely " scriptural " considerations, to the reconciling
of Christian doctrine and narrative with the nature of
things ; and here his logic is necessarily mere quibbling.
But we reach something worse than quibbling when we
come to his reconciliation of the fact of the existence
of sin with his dogma of a punishing deity.

It was meet [he writes] *if* Sin *did* come into existence, and appear
in the world, it should arise from the imperfection which *properly*
belongs to a creature, as such, and *should appear to do so*, that it
might *appear* not to be from God as the efficient or fountain.   But
this could not have been, if man *had* been made at first with Sin
in his heart ; nor unless the abiding principle and habit of Sin
were first *introduced by an evil act of the creature.*   If sin had not
arose from the imperfection of the creature, it *would not have been
so visible* that it did not arise from God as the positive cause and
real source of it.

Here we have one of the acutest of reasoners committing one of the grossest conceivable confusions of
argument.   Not only does he here flatly negate his own
main doctrine, he relapses into sheer nullity of phrase.
The whole point of the passage is that as Sin *evidently
did* arise " by an evil act of the creature," *therefore* it
must have done so.   On that simple plan, the argument
could have been stopped by an opponent at any stage :
the Arminian had only to say that men's wills are

---

[1] His formula of virtue as " benevolence towards all being," by
the way, was put before him, in almost his words, by Bishop
Cumberland.

evidently not predetermined, and therefore cannot have been. And Edwards, hypnotised as he is at this point by his dogmatics, feels that something is wrong, for he goes on to protest that, as regards the objections of the Arminians,

> No additional difficulty is incurred by adhering to a scheme in this manner differing from theirs, and none would be removed or avoided by agreeing with and maintaining theirs. Nothing that the Arminians say about the contingence or self-determining power of man's will can serve to explain, with less difficulty, how the first sinful volition of mankind could take place, and man be justly charged with the blame of it.

This is quite true : all theists are in the same dilemma ; and on theistic lines the strife of Calvinism and Arminianism is absolutely insoluble. But that is the condemnation of both. The rational solution is one that annihilates the whole theistic premisses. All of them alike—Creation, Foreordination, Infinite Goodness, Infinite Justice, Grace, Original Sin, and Eternal Punishment—are pure counter-senses, the result of applying the categories of the finite and relative to the concept of the All ; and they held their place in such a mind as that of Edwards, as they do in weaker minds to this day, in virtue of the capacity of man to be hypnotised by traditionary error—call it Myth, Religion, Authority, or what you will. *Tantum relligio potuit suadere malorum.*

To-day, a mind of such power as belonged to that of Edwards, so placed as to be fairly open from childhood onwards to rational influences, could not hold his creed ; could not stand with him on the doctrine of the sin and fall of Adam, and the consequent predeterminate " guilt " of the whole human race, to the point of justifying the dogma of infant damnation. It was the peculiar emotional habit set up by early and continuous superinduced hysteria on Christian lines that so warped such an intelligence. Had he even met in his youth with the *Ethica* of Spinoza, where are set forth so many of his arguments on will, he might have been emancipated by the one penetrating thought, *ad Dei naturam neque intellectum neque voluntatem pertinere,* " to the nature of God neither intellect nor will pertains." [1] That indeed is not a final deliverance from the fallacy

[1] *Ethica*, Pt. I, Prop. xvii, Schol. Propp. xxxi, xxxii.

of theism ; for Spinoza himself, while thus logically excluding from his doctrine of the Infinite those finite modes, proceeds, in affirming the necessary determination of all things, to ascribe to the infinite " omnipotence "—all-powerful*ness*, a mere abstraction of the idea of force with " All," and " capacity for " superadded. He might as well have affirmed " All-will." In the infinite indeed inheres all force, but the abstraction " all-forcefulness " is a mere verbalism ; and the " he " of Spinoza is a perpetual paralogism.

Great, however, was the moral gain from the great step Spinoza did take, for in his ethic does the better spirit of humanity first begin to find its coherently reasoned justification. Hitherto the best instincts of men had been overridden by creeds which divinised the ethic of savagery, placing beside the ordinance of compassion the dogma of retribution. The paralogism of a Good God had lent itself to every cruelty, the animal bias of men glorifying and sanctioning itself by attributing to Infinity its own appetite for protracted revenge, and its own expedients of imprisonment and torture. The whole of that evil ethic followed on the irrational conception of Infinity as a Will, a Creator, a Governing Person, who hated and punished sin. Thus have religious people, at all times, with the best intentions, as the phrase goes, been worsening life with the idea of bettering it, shutting a door on moral progress by way of terrifying sinners into righteousness.

When once we substitute for the irrational conception of a Personal Infinite the rational conception of universal causation or causal sequence, the problem of morals presents no difficulties save those (certainly numerous) involved in being consistent despite of tradition or bias and habit. We recognise at once that men vary congenitally in moral bias and capacity as in every other respect. Where the theologian, in defiance of the whole spectacle of life, insists that the worst evil-doers *know* they do evil precisely as others know it, making at most a grudging and inconsistent exception in favour of the unquestionably insane, the naturalist recognises many degrees of moral incapacity from " insanity " to quasi-perfection. It is the theological habit of charging men with " sinning against the light " that involves men

in such absurdities : they will not surrender the carnal
joy which such denunciation gives them. I have heard
a theologian thus publicly declare that a criminal who
manifestly took pleasure in atrocious murders knew
perfectly well how criminal he was ; and a number of
theists, thus fooled to the top of their bent, applauded
him. Such words, to mean anything in terms of consciousness, must mean that the criminal in question
found his crimes as loathsome to enact as we should find
them, yet went on committing them because he chose
to do so. Here we have the inveterate absurdity of the
moral absolutist.

It will not, I hope, put you to much trouble to be
met by the old parry of the theologian, to the effect
that, though there are many cogent arguments in favour
of the causedness of volition, yet they are set aside by
the primordial fact that, nevertheless, " we know [or
feel] that we are free to will." It is the fact, however,
that this argument has given trouble to some ostensibly
non-theological reasoners, as Professor Fowler, and even
to Professor Sidgwick. The former has said [1] that the
conflict between the feeling of liberty of volition and
the unanswerable arguments for determinism is insoluble,
because determinism in his view excludes praise and
blame, which are nevertheless irreducible ; and the latter
has avowed similar difficulty, only professing [2] to offer
a " practical solution " by way of the avowal that we
" cannot use determinist conceptions " when we are
making a choice. It may be well, then, to put briefly
the logical solution of their difficulties.

With the question of praise and blame I shall deal
later : meantime let us note first how both Professors
miscarry because they had never looked to their logical
fundamentals. Had they done so they would have
noted that the verbal predications of " freedom " and
" unfreedom " can have no rational bearing singly on
the absolute category of volitions, inasmuch as they are
admittedly not *both* applicable ; and that accordingly
the impossibility of " using a determinist conception "
when making a choice is no more of a philosophical

---

[1] *Principles of Morals*, pt. ii, 336.
[2] Article on " Some Fundamental Ethical Controversies," in
Mind, October, 1889.

difficulty than the impossibility of applying to choice the concept of extension, or to light the concept of gravitation. But as Professor Sidgwick had missed this consideration, he would probably not have been convinced by it; and to one in his position we should have to put the matter *a posteriori*. As thus. It is only at first sight that our volitions seem even to common-sense to be " free "; for if Professor Sidgwick had been invited to commit a series of murders for gain he would have found in his moral bias to the contrary an invincible force. Even if, however, this bias be itself defined as a volition, a choice, and the " difficulty " thus reasserted, the shock of the logic of determinism is to be got over just as is the shock of discovering that the rising and setting of the sun are only apparent motions of the sun. When I decide to take a walk I certainly do not " use " the scientific conception of the gravitation of my body towards the earth's centre, or that of the rotation of the earth on its axis, because those conceptions have nothing to do with my purpose. My " common-sense " knows of no downward pull upon me, because my whole existence is conditioned by that downward pull; and it knows of no whirling of the earth, precisely because of my physical relation to the earth. But who has now any difficulty in acknowledging the gravitation and the rotation?

At first, no doubt, it was otherwise: to most men of the sixteenth century the doctrine of Copernicus seemed utter folly; and even to this day we practically do not " use " the conception of gravitation for a single act, though men of science use it for research into the processes of the cosmos. But simple familiarity with the conception excludes all sense of " difficulty "; and it will be just the same when men have become rationally familiar with the conception of determinism. As we move *in* gravitation or rest *in* the earth's movement, we choose *in* the process of determination. Satisfaction in this view is substantially a matter of habit of mind: as Mill put it, " what persons can and what they cannot conceive is very much an affair of accident." [1] We shall not say that we are " free " to will any more than that we are " free " to fly or to live under water. We

---

[1] *System of Logic*, B. iii, c. v, § ii: 1-vol. ed., p. 237.

shall continue to say that we are or desire to be free to *act as we will or would*, having willed in terms of motives. Thinkers who are still at Professor Sidgwick's point of view would do well to go back to Locke's query whether anybody wants to be " free " to will without any motive or bias.

And the moral gain from the explicit acceptance of the law of causation in volition is this, that just as the conception of gravitation immensely advances our comprehension of the relations of our earth to the cosmos, so the conception of determinism immensely advances our comprehension of our moral relations to each other ; or rather, let us say, it visibly will so advance us. Step by step the theologian has been driven from the insane ethic of infant damnation, the insane practices of heretic-burning and witch-burning, the blind cruelty of torturing witnesses and flogging madmen, to a relative sanity and decency of method. But we are still, in Emerson's phrase, " at cockcrow and the morning star." The late Dr. Martineau, a too eloquent apostle of bias, was wont to argue that the determinist view of life altered its whole moral dynamics. In a sense (the expression is too loose to be fixable) it will do that ; but only gradually, even for the determinist ; and the in-determinist is still to reckon with. When the reasoner urges on the man of instinct that all volition is determined by capacity, training, and circumstances ; that all punishment is mere animalism unless it be rationally calculated to work reformation, and that most punishment actually does not and cannot work reformation, the man of instinct throws up new defences—certain sophists and certain imperfect reasoners helping him—in the shape of (1) protests that such rationalism takes away the sense of " responsibility," and (2) questions as to how we continue to bestow praise and blame, to feel admiration or repulsion, or to be capable of remorse. Here, as we have seen, a thinker quite friendly to determinism, Professor Fowler, capitulates to the difficulty. " For the last enemy to be destroyed is fallacy."

By this time, however, you (I hope) will have little difficulty in defending yourselves against the new assault of verbalisms. " Responsibility " is a general synonym for duty, either explicitly accepted or legally and generally imposed. Responsibility on the part of a " creature " to its alleged " creator," of the clay to the potter, is unthinkable : as well talk of the responsibility of a bullet to a gun, or to the marksman. Such an idea is one more application of a category of discrimination to an absolute series without its correlatives. But on the part of man towards man there are responsibilities general and special ; and inasmuch as all men are on one plane (with endless diversities of capacity and opportunity) as regards the determinateness of their wills, each has the right, in general, to make contracts with others, and all collectively have the right to frame laws for the equal protection of all. By " have the right " I mean that so to act is in consistency with the most generally accepted of all moral propositions—that we ought to do as we would be done by, or, more strictly, ought not to do what we know we should resent having done to us. Difficulties begin to arise round that principle when we consider the case of the wrongdoer who would like to be left unblamed ; and we proceed to solve them by framing rules in what seem to be the general interest, deciding that he who commits an initial aggression on another is fitly to be restrained or deterred.

And now comes more clearly into view the immense moral superiority of the ethic of reason over the ethic of religion. While the traditions and devices of barbarism are accepted as " revelation," and fortified by the fallacies of theism, it is held that he who does wrong must be made to suffer *because* " sin ought to be punished " —that is to say, the proposition is merely restated in terms of revelation and primitive instinct. The theist of to-day is content merely to confine the offending madman as not being " responsible," but is still resolute to make the bad man suffer. Now, so far as we know, madman and bad man differ only in this, that the one's brain is diseased or injured, and the other's is congenitally ill-balanced. It may be argued, indeed, that the dependence of mind on brain is " only an inference," not a certainty ; but unless we are to revert to the Arminian chimæra of a personality without bias or predisposition, we must at least say that the bad man is somehow predisposed to evil. Rationally stated, then, the problem is this : Is the badness such as is proved to constitute an intolerable risk to society ; and if yes, how shall society best be protected ? Given alternative modes of protection, that is rationally to be preferred which causes *least* suffering to the wrongdoer, unless the other would (*a*) demonstrably tend to reform him, or (*b*) burden society unduly—two problems calling for much careful calculation.

To act otherwise is to be intellectually inconsistent, and temperamentally brutal. If all evil-doing *ought* to entail suffering, the madman should not escape : indeed, it is probable that some admitted madmen are to some extent more amenable to threats and suffering than some certificated " sane " criminals. But why, seeing evil done and suffering caused, should I seek *therefore* to cause more suffering ? The instinct in that direction is no rational pretext : like the instinct of the criminal himself it is sheer animalism : only the hope of *doing good* can rationalise an act of retribution. Now, the question as to how far punishments have ever done good or may be made to do so, either by reforming offenders or " deterring others," is one of social art, so to speak ; one of comparison and research, of sociology and psychology. Having discussed it elsewhere, I shall not occupy you with it here : the essential point in this connection is that we are bound in reason thus to substitute the conception of human utility for the conception of that duty of social revenge in the name of Deity which is argued for by the very people who affirm the same Deity's prohibition of individual revenge, and quote the text, " Vengeance is mine, saith the Lord." By putting all such insincerities aside, we are capacitated to combine compassion with self-preservation, to act as rational believers in the causation of all conduct without fore-going a single means of influencing conduct for the better.

This last claim you may hear denied by those who say that the doctrine of determinism must tend to corrupt character by teaching men to regard their weaknesses and vices as incurable. Now, if that were true, mankind must long ago have been corrupted beyond remedy by the doctrine of the Infinite and All-Good Creator. Some measure of such corruption has doubtless taken place.[1] But such is the natural instinct of men to self-esteem and to hope for betterment, that, though bad men may have caught at predestination as a formal excuse for their sins, and some are bewildered by theology into antinomianism, men of average character seem almost always to count on becoming better either by " grace " or by good resolutions. And while a weak theist may be argued into recklessness by a propounder of predestination, no sane rationalist can be moved to " give way " to his worse propensities by the mere thought that they are innate, when all the while he knows his better tendencies are equally innate. Nothing can prove that he is determinate to a given end until that end is reached : his volition is always the point of determination ; and in the terms of the case his next volition is unknown ; the die is never cast, so to speak, till it no longer matters how he argues. When a man has lost hope for betterment the machine is already out of gear.

So obvious is this that the opponents of determinism are fain to fall back on another plea. Granted, they say—and, as we said, they can quote the admission of a would-be determinist on their side—granted that a determinist is not shut up to inanition on his own part by his belief, at least he is shut up in consistency to abstaining from praise and blame of others, thus losing a powerful means of affecting others for the better. This again is pure fallacy, the correlative of the fallacy about responsibility. What we have affirmed about conduct is its causation : now, the recognition of causation in an aspect of *physical* nature has never withheld men from the language of praise, though (and this is hopefully significant) it has withheld them from the language of moral blame. We " praise " beauty in a landscape, we praise beauty in a face—though not to the beautiful person, save in circumstances which I need not detail. If, then, we take avowed joy in the sight of physical beauty, knowing that it is predeterminate in the person as in the landscape, what should con-

[1] Rabanus Maurus, for instance, declared that the teaching of Gottschalk had driven many people to moral despair, and others to reckless licence (cited by Waddington, *Hist. of the Church*, 1833, p. 259, *n.*).

ceivably withhold us from taking avowed joy in the sight of goodness, moral beauty, seeing that there is practically no restriction of prudence or taste—save by way of expression—on the avowal ? Praise is fundamentally the expression of pleasure : it is only on theological presuppositions that moral praise is made to seem something else.

As regards blame, again, where is the trouble ? The plea of causation is indeed a rational rebuttal to cruelty, to mere vengeance ; and so much the better ; but it is no bar to self-preservation. The most devoted champion of the indeterminateness of the human will will grant that a tiger is rather plainly predisposed to prey ; but will probably not go on to say that because the tiger is thus " not responsible " we ought to let him eat us. It is the same with a thug or a thief : our right of self-preservation is primordial, and no argument can undermine it. And so, in degree, with blame. Certainly the consistent determinist (no easy thing to be, I confess) will withhold blame where he believes blame can do no good, just as a physician will not scold a lunatic, or even (at the moment of diagnosis) a fever-patient. But where he has reason to think blame *can* do good, where, feeling wronged, he may reasonably reckon on making the wronger realise his injustice and inconsistency, his blame is as rational as it is spontaneous. That he should control his expression of it by his sense of purpose—whether to influence the wrongdoer or to counteract his tendencies by warning others—is pure moral gain. And where, finally, we recognise that he who wrongs us or others is too badly biased to be influenced by our blame, we have one of two courses rationally open to us. Either the wrongdoer is liable to restraint under law or he is not. If he is, verbal blame is superfluous : the " punishment " is blame put in action ; and the scoldings administered by judges to offenders in the act of decreeing punishment on them are neither rational nor seemly.

If, again, the wrongdoing is of a kind that is not provided for by law (and sometimes even if it is !) our rational course is either to keep aloof from the offender, thereby expressing our blame with tolerably practical emphasis, or, if from compassion or a higher sense of duty we go on enduring his society, to show by our natural sadness or restraint what we feel. Beyond this, on no reasonable pretence can we be called upon to go. No more than we can go into raptures over physical ugliness can we feel happiness or trustful comradeship in the presence of moral deformity; nor does the principle of determinism commit us to pretending that we do. With an ugly person, certainly, we are committed by good feeling and right reason to suppressing all sign of discomfort: to do otherwise would be to inflict avoidable suffering with no compensating gain. With an insane person we act as does the physician, for the reason last given as well as out of compassion. But with a bad person we feel distrust; and as the indication of this is the last chance of influencing him for good, we are under no duty whatever of restraining it, save as regards " economy " or the judicious expression of it. The rationale of the matter is—I will not say, as clear as on the theistic view: it is incomparably clearer.

Yet I have heard a distinguished clerical writer childishly argue that on the determinist view all praise and blame must amount to a mere " moral stratagem," as who should say that it is a stratagem to smile with pleasure, or to wince when you burn your hand; and there may still be in circulation in your day a work in which a statesman of to-day [1] argues, just as childishly, to my thinking, that a determinist cannot rationally feel remorse for wrongdoing. It is as if one should say that a determinist cannot rationally be sorry to find he has cancer, or because he was born with a club foot. Mr. Balfour, it is true, tries to give a philosophic aspect to his argument by urging that we cannot enjoy beauty of colour or sound unless we conceive such beauty as something akin to a transcendental beauty somewhere perceived by a transcendental mind; and that for that kind of reason we shall fail to discriminate with praise and blame between either moral or physical charm and ugliness when we conceive them all as equally determinate moments in the infinite whole. But until Mr. Balfour can assure or convince us that he enjoys his dinner only because he thinks a transcendental power

[1] Mr. Balfour (afterwards Earl Balfour) in his *Foundations of Belief.*

transcendently enjoys transcendental meals, I shall take leave to regard his argument as the most remarkable display of philosophic insincerity made in my time.

These devices of theological polemic, you will note, are all instances of the fallacy of applying relative terms singly to unrelated categories, affirming one term of a contrast singly of an uncontrasted series, to the exclusion of the other term. Did men reason rigorously, such fallacies could never arise ; but even a loose reasoner, were he not fixed in his presupposition, would see the futility of arguing that determinism ought logically to make us indifferent to our moral conditions, as being determinate, while tacitly recognising that it cannot conceivably make us indifferent to our physical conditions, which are equally determinate. The sophism is indeed doubly absurd, for, in the very terms of the determinist case, we start from a moral *bias*, which is the negation of moral indifference. The anti-determinist in effect says, Because you believe you have a bias, you ought not to have a bias. Such ultimate absurdities come of the spirit of partisanship, against which I have before warned you. All the while, the partisan here is on other grounds committed, like theologians in general, to the doctrine of foreordination in its theistic form : he oppugns it simply when it is stated in its non-theistic form ; in which case he will not scruple to negate causation. Now it is precisely the theist who is stultified when he condemns any aspect of things, moral or physical, since his most solemn and most general doctrine is that all things happen by God's holy will, under which they work together for good. It has been repeatedly declared that the essence of religion is submission to the omnipotent divine will. But the primordial figment commits its acceptor to perpetual inconsequence : in the name of religion he is to be remorseful for certain of his own acts which are alleged to reverse the omnipotent divine will, and he is to condemn other men's acts on the same score even when accepting them as part of that will. For the naturalist there is no counter-sense of divine will in the case, and there is no inconsequence in his rational relation to the order of things. He resists moral evil as he resists physical evil, on the score that

F

his own moral judgment, playing on all the knowledge he can attain, is for him at each moment the crowning stage of moral volition in the cosmos.

We can now solve without difficulty the old problem as to whether the man most to be admired is he who has no evil propensities to resist, or he who has them, but in general or finally overcomes them. Our admiration is properly the expression of our pleasure after due reflection, and we can take no pleasure in the thought that anyone has evil propensities. What we do is to rejoice with him when he overcomes them—as, for instance, when a man with a bias to alcoholism is so moved by his perception of the harm it does, or by the blame or contempt or appeals addressed to him, as to acquire a stronger bias, controlling the first. To rejoice with him is not to say he is a better man than one quite soundly constituted ; but, on the other hand, for the determinist to say that he is a faultier man is not to raise any question of his liability to either punishment or reward : it is to bring his controlled propensity into line with a lameness, as a thing calling for compassion or sympathy and no longer for blame, though blame, intelligently adjusted, may again become fitting if the propensity reasserts itself.

Long as this letter has grown, I must not end it without reverting to that old theorem which we have seen employed by Hegel to vindicate theism—the theorem, namely, that " evil is *non-ens* " or " not positive." The thought is one that still appeals to earnest and reflective people ; but you will see on a moment's consideration that it is wholly beside the problems of morals, and that it is but a half-thought at best. It was employed by such a gifted thinker as John the Scot, who got it from earlier thinkers, to solve the old dilemma of God's authorship of evil ; and it is so employed still. But the whole procedure is stamped with fallacy, for it is precisely the *existence* of evil that sets men on thus verbally proving its non-existence. In some forms of the argument, as in that put by Shaftesbury in his *Characteristics*, we are told that evil is so only to us : from the point of view of the Infinite it is not evil. So be it. Then by the very same reasoning good is *non-ens* : it is good only to us ; from the point of view of the Infinite it is not good. We are at the old futility of turning the explicitly relative into an attribute of the All.

You will agree with me, I think, that " the point of view of the Infinite " is not a point at which the finite can place itself ; and that the verbalising semblance of doing so, whatever gymnastic value the process may have, will certainly not help morals, save insofar as it may help men to realise the very truth we have been discussing, that conduct is a form of cosmic causation. As we have seen, however, the normal effect of supposing you are at the point of view of the Infinite has not been to make men either sane or merciful. Remember that all those disputes as to the punishability of men by their Maker did not arise by way of sequent reasoning from the concept of Infinity : they arose as attempts to justify a barbaric conception of a " future life " in which good people are to be ostentatiously rewarded and bad people brutally punished, just as on earth. It is because for ages men have set out on the path of philosophy thus burdened with the credences of ancestral ignorance that they have so constantly stumbled. The burden was one of bad morals as well as of bad logic ; and it belongs to the situation that the bad morals should help to keep the logic bad. The more reason to feel assured that right reasoning, when they attain to it, will infallibly make them better men. To believe otherwise is to believe that insincerity promotes virtue ; for to insincerity, as we have defined it, we always come in our analysis of logical error.

Let me here avow once more, however, that the risk of insincerity is not all on one side. What I mean by the word, in the special force I have given it, will often be chargeable on the rationalist—on me, on you. For even as the supernaturalist is caught in the spell of a strong " will to believe," which commits him to insincerities of argument, so are we all apt to be held in the net of an instinctive tendency that is rebel to our reason, and plays it false. No instinct is more spontaneous than that of blame, of retribution : even those of us who instinctively recoil from such a " revenge " as aims deliberately at injuring an enemy for vengeance' sake are open to the satisfactions of severe censure ; and few there be who scientifically adjust their blame to the remedial or self-guarding purposes which ought in reason to control it. No one, I think, can do so at all times : we all vary in our capacity to be judicial ; and I confess to finding the difficulty constant at this point. That is to say, I find myself frequently lapsing into " insincerity " as I have defined it, in that my reasoned conviction and my act do not consist.

The inconsistency, as you will see, is not at all that charged by those who deny to the determinist the right to praise and blame at all : that charge we have seen to be pure paralogism. It lies in the non-restriction of praise and blame, but much more particularly blame, to our reasoned perception of its fitness, of its utility. We are inconsistent, insincere, not when we call the bad man bad, or the thief a thief, or the liar a liar, still less (if possible) when we repent of having ourselves done a cruel or a faithless act, but when we merely vilify and humiliate the liar without seeking to do good, or add insult and ill-usage and hard antipathy to our imprisonment of the thief. It is when we merely gratify our resentment, in an animal temper, that we are false to our avowed recognition of the causedness of the resented action, the determination of will by antecedents. If, when attacked by a mad dog or any wild beast, I should do any more than defend myself to the extent of killing the animal, if I should seek to enjoy revenge by keeping it in a state of protracted torture, I should prove myself more of an animal, so to speak, than of a thinking man. It is the same with human offences. If we resent them further than (1) to safeguard ourselves, (2) to affect the offender for the better by making him either afraid or sorry, or (3) to put others on their guard against him, we are, as determinists, insincere : we are approximating to the sophisticated cruelties of the theologian.

Doubtless the keen resentment of iniquity and baseness which has underlain much theological denunciation of sin may be justified on the third of the grounds I have just given : it stirs up the better feelings of the spectators, turns what might have remained apathy into an antipathy that involves sympathy with the right, and reveals to some dull intelligences *their* past inconsistency. At times such an utterance of blame, as it seems to me, is the most pressing of public duties; and when it involves much more unpopularity than applause there is a certain presumption that, if done with sanity and competence, it is not a mere gratification of malice. But remember that where the theologian's moral philosophy ends the rationalist's should as such begin; and that, if you do not rest on judgment where he rests on instinct and fiction, you are in a fair way to be as insincere as he.

When all is said, perhaps, your best advantage over him will be in the power to detect and check your insincerities. I do not mean that he does not do this: his literature is full of avowals of backsliding and unworthiness. But these very avowals he will instantly disavow when it is a question of accrediting his creed and discrediting " unbelief " : it is his doom to be for ever at the mercy of his false premisses. Delivered from those premisses, ours should be the happier as it is the clearer case. But part of its happiness will consist, not in any sense of superiority (that is a poor stay for normal comfort; nay, a sure source of intellectual demoralisation, though it may be the supreme stay in a moral struggle), but in the perpetual reminder of the critical reason that in respect of the primary snare of insincerity we are all kin; that where we ourselves have reached, all may one day be; and that there is thus no limit in man's nature to a perpetual betterment.

LETTER X

IN reading the foregoing letters it may have occurred to you at times that I seem to give a very low place to "instinct," and, again, that I finally accept it as the ultimate discriminator between good and evil, the determinant of virtue and wickedness. I recognise that there is something there to be cleared up. Unless we logically solve the apparent contradiction, there will remain a possible source of much confusion in argument on moral questions.

From the discussion on the so-called freedom of the will we reached the conclusion that a general moral bias underlies all our moral judgments; that people are in large measure born predisposed to become good or bad; and that a varying degree of susceptibility to given motives constitutes in large part the "determination" of our wills. When we see people with a marked cast of benevolence or of cruelty, of truthfulness or of the reverse, albeit similarly educated and situated, we recognise this clearly enough. But even in the discussion on these moral problems which hinge on that of the causation of will, we could not but see that moral bias is set up by doctrinal training; and we are reminded that it is also set up by mere associations, and that a special set of temptations may further make all the difference between the outbreak and the control of the worse forms of "instinct" in many persons. Nay, we have proof that certain kinds of physical shock or damage to the brain may greatly alter a man's bias or balance, even turning a good character into a bad one. All the while the "determination" of the will is clear; but what exactly are we to understand by "instinct" in these different aspects?

Let us clear the position point by point. The determinist argument commits us to Hume's position (implicit in those of some theists before him, as Cumberland and Edwards), that in every enquiry into the bases of morals we come finally to a " sentiment," a feeling, a bias, which cannot further be analysed.[1] That sentiment or bias is a determination of our wills. If we like very much to help people, why, we like it ; if we like very much to hurt them, there is no getting away from that fact, whether or not we are at the same time sufficiently cautious to keep clear of the criminal law. But it is also a fact that strong moral volitions or dispositions of feeling may be developed by a course of training, and that the special bias so shaped is to the mind that feels it indistinguishable at bottom from any other kind of moral judgment.

We may say, indeed, that some " instincts " are primary, and others superinduced. Thus all men like to have their own way ; and it would be an enormously difficult thing to train anybody to enjoy being kicked, though some slaves may perhaps be made tolerably callous to the sensation. But whereas in a free country, as the phrase goes, a feeling of indignation at the act of kicking an " inferior " may be practically universal, the inhabitant of a free country may after a short residence in Egypt or parts of South Africa become quite complacent over such an act, whether done by himself or by others. The well-bred Englishman, coming unexpectedly on a scene of servant-kicking for the first time, will recoil from it, and the recoil will have to his own mind all the aspects of " instinct " ; but the Englishman who kicks is feeling and acting just as instinctively. We arrive at this generalisation, that we all resent or dislike that act or judgment which sharply conflicts with our judgment, but that our judgment is largely alterable by training and circumstances.

In Mark Twain's admirable story, " Huckleberry Finn," there is a capital picture of the state of mind of the boy who feels that he is doing a " low-down " thing in helping a negro slave, the property of a friend of his, to escape. A boy brought up to think slavery an infamous wrong would have a quite contrary feeling in the same case : he would feel he was doing a praise-worthy act, and be jubilant. Each boy would be ex-

[1] Appendix I to *Enquiry Concerning the Principles of Morals.*

hibiting moral feeling and a fairly conscientious cast of mind, the first no less than the second : nay, the first boy *might* be at bottom the better of the two, might be in general more trustworthy, more kind-hearted. Apart from such a superiority, the difference between them is to be recognised as one of moral education ; and the same verdict holds good of the widely divergent sentiments of multitudes of people respectively born in slave-holding and " free " countries. But on the other hand there have grown up in slave-holding communities a certain number of people who revolted at slavery, and in free countries a number of people who either positively sympathised with the slave-holders or cared nothing about the matter ; such persons in both cases coming to their conclusions in virtue of a primary bias, not being led to their views by their teachers. Here we note a specially marked determination of moral feeling or of insensibility, a special cast of sympathy or of unimaginativeness. To sum up, so far, some men strike us by their bias, others, so to speak, by their biasableness—both phenomena being of course forms of determination of the will. Whether I grow up markedly disposed to gentleness or to cruelty, or markedly open to persuasion by those about me, either way I exhibit predisposition.

It begins to be clear, then, that we can make concerning " instinct " what we have otherwise seen to be a rational or logical proposition, that it may be *either* good *or* bad, best or worst. We can broadly say with Kant that there is nothing better than a good will, that is, a bias to good—by which, of course, we do not mean that such a will may not be bettered by increase of knowledge. Rather, we realise that instinct is variously subject to modification by training and by reflection on freshly seen truths ; and, in particular, that our (instinctive) judgment as to what *is* good or bad in instinct is modifiable by training and knowledge, though every new moral argument in turn works down to a basis of feeling. In other words, *instinct is modifiable in terms of instinct*, in the sense that all reasoning is a complex of feelings, that all feeling relates to knowledge, and that new knowledge means new feeling. Always a man seeks that which he likes or wants : in that primary sense we are all egoists. But some of us like or want to help others to *their* satisfactions; and this sort of egoism differentiates sharply from that which cares little for other people's happiness. To that, accordingly, we restrict the name in its censorious sense. And yet that narrow and self-regarding egoism *may* expand towards the large and altruistic, in virtue of the sheer fact of desire for satisfactions.

Now for our ethical crux. If all moral judgments thus root in feeling or " sentiment " or bias, it follows that there may be irreducible conflicts of moral feeling. If, for instance, a man is so constituted as positively to enjoy torturing animals, his pleasure therein will make him insusceptible to my protest that he is exhibiting a low animal passion, unless indeed he happens to be still more susceptible to the pain of blame; and he may meet me with my own proposition that a fundamental feeling is the last standard of right and wrong. Similarly a theologian may tell me that he *feels* that sin ought to be punished, and that from this feeling there is no appeal. Now, it should at once be admitted that a certain degree of strength of bias is not alterable by argument, and that if an opponent is not affected in his fundamental feeling by our argument, the argument as against him has failed. What follows? This: that the moral ideals and teachings struggle for survival, and gain or lose adherents in virtue of their greater or lesser attractiveness, or conformity to interest and bias. A community will readily accept a moral code which sanctions what most of the community want to do, unless it thereby chances to bring into clear relief their inconsistency by affirming something that they usually deny. In that case many will disavow the code while acting on it. The whole chance for good morals lies in this, that at bottom and in the long run it is *useful* for the mass of men to do as they would be done by. But inasmuch as it so often seems useful to the individual or the community as such to do otherwise, the fortunes of morality depend proximately on the variations of moral bias. That is to say, a great gift for consistency or for comprehension of the true interests of society is a " variation " of the nature of genius; and though the men who constitute such moral variations in the human species do not survive in virtue of their goodness, they may so persuade a community as to secure by changed action a marked increase in happiness, in which case their superior ethic gains ground, and tends to become the " instinctive " form of judgment of the average persons who would otherwise have judged differently.

Thus the higher morality prospers simply as a variation towards higher rationality, for it is only through appeals to the instincts for truth, consistency, and betterment that the average will is to be brought from a lower to a higher choice. It is quite true that, while the theologian *feels* he ought to make the lives of criminals miserable in prison, he is impervious to the arguments which prove the contrary ; and while any man feels only or mainly in terms of primary egoism he cannot be made a good man (in terms of *our* feeling) by any reasoned demonstration. But experience shows that by degrees the better types of theologian can be enlightened by knowledge and argument to the point of feeling differently about punishment, present and future ; and it is historically very certain that as regards the criminal and primary egotistic types we are not a whit worse off as determinists than our fathers were as theists. The failure of supernaturalist ethic and practice to lessen crime and to promote sympathy is written over the whole surface of history : it is stupendous ; and so far as experience has yet gone everything tends to show that a scientific handling of moral problems will give immeasurably better results than the theological ever did.

Broadly speaking, progress in morals consists in extension of sympathy ; and though sympathy is not co-extensive with knowledge, it is clear enough that in general extended knowledge is the way to extended sympathy. Genius for sympathy is rare : most of us depend for advance there on culture and widened experience. And if it be true that to do as we would be done by is to máximise well-being, then the more ready people are to act on that principle the better the world will be.

Here, of course, we take for granted that such betterment is *felt* to be a desirable thing. With anyone who does not or cannot be led to feel it, there is no arguing :

we can but seek to discredit him, and, if need be, restrain his anti-social acts.   His is the egoism we are driven to regard as evil : if it cannot be transmuted by the appeal to consistency or by the experience of retaliation in kind, it is to be reckoned with as an anti-social appetite. But a fresh confusion is being set up in ethics by some who, reverting to the test of total utility as between conflicting forms of bias, wholly or partially repudiate on that score the rule of doing as we would be done by.   We are to consider, they say, whether a given act will advantage society in the future : if we can show that it will, it is thereby justified, even if in achieving it we do to non-aggressors what we should greatly resent having done to us.   As commonly put, this argument is limited to acts by the community as such : I have not seen any professed student of morals openly argue that the individual will do well to act on the same principle ; and this restriction of the thesis is significant. If the principle be sound, it surely ought to be laid down for all action.   That it is suggested only as a code for communities is apparently due either to a lack of sincere belief in it on the part of those who urge it, or to the perception that, while an unrestricted form of the pro- position would get a man into trouble as encouraging crime, the restricted form will keep him on good terms with a community that is disposed collectively to do otherwise than as it would be done by.

Now, this teaching is not sufficiently disposed of by merely insisting that the law of reciprocity is primary and unchallengeable, though we may hope that one day it will be felt to be so.   If our ethic is to be rational we must be prepared to meet all reasoned opposition ; and if it be argued that civilisation is to be bettered by our ceasing in any set of cases to do as we would be done by, we must see what the argument is worth.   A common illustration of the theory is the case of ancient slavery. It seems on retrospect that the possession of slaves was a means of leisure to studious men, and it is in- ferred that slavery thus made possible a development of letters, arts, and sciences which otherwise could not have taken place.   Those developments, in turn, being passed on to posterity, have greatly promoted human happiness in ages which have been able to abolish slavery.

Ergo, it is urged, slavery is not always or necessarily wrong. Here we have a very interesting problem in sociology, and an important exercise in reasoning.

The problem, you will see, is twofold, and the proposition before us recognises only one of its aspects. First we have to ask, what constitutes a wrong ? next, what *would* have happened in antiquity had there been no slavery ? On the first head we say that a wrong act is in the first place a departure from an agreed-on code, wrongdoing being a relation between man and man. Now, all communities have agreed among themselves to certain necessary restrictions or definitions of the law of reciprocity, notably the provisions for dealing with theft, fraud, and violence. We do not say : " If I stole, I should like to be let off ; therefore I shall let off thieves " ; we agree rather to affirm that thieving is an act we shall never commit, and consequently one in respect of which we shall never desire reciprocity : and as it is on the other hand seen to be an intolerable aggression on society, we agree to " punish " or otherwise resist it. But in many communities the systematic definition of the law of reciprocity has gone much farther than this ; and in those of antiquity it went to the length of permitting men (*a*) to sell themselves into slavery in payment of gambling debts or for other considerations, (*b*) to sell their children, and (*c*) to enslave and sell captives and the children of captives.

Now, it is not to be denied that, given these legal practices, slavery could not anciently have figured as a " wrong " in the sense in which it does for us to-day. Men's relation towards it was rather such as our relation to (*a*) cases in which men are ruined by paying gambling debts, (*b*) cases in which the children of a ruined or dead man are left to sink from comfort to poverty, and (*c*) the innumerable cases in which men see others suffer from poverty and do nothing to help them beyond giving small alms or supplying public " relief." To most of us to-day this degree of apathy seems natural and fitting, while the ancient apathy on the subject of slavery seems strange or even revolting. I hope, and I hold it likely, that one day our apathies will seem to our posterity strange and revolting, and that it will be held a matter of course that no one shall under any circum-

stances be left to suffer physically from poverty ; that
mere poverty, in fact, will be socially made impossible ;
and that in particular the acceptance of a " gambling
debt " which can impoverish anyone will be regarded
as an odious action. On this view, you see, moral
judgments are very clearly " relative," varying from age
to age ; and we may at once agree that it is misleading
to speak of ancient slavery as if its maintenance stood
for relatively the same degree of moral apathy as the
maintenance of slavery would imply to-day.

Let us not forget, however, that the ancients were
just as much liable to " insincerity " as we ; and let us
not hesitate to suppose that Aristotle, for instance, was
insincere when he met as he did the protests of the
more sympathetic men of his time against slavery.[1]
The fact was that those men represented a variation
towards a higher moral instinct than his, a larger sympathy, a greater capacity for the " good life " at which
he professed to aim. I at least cannot doubt that he
was, as we say, false to his lights, that he fell back on
his habits, his prejudice, and would not reduce his doctrine to consistency. With his large and lucid intelligence, he could see that the Platonists were inconsistent
in justifying the enslavement of captives and opposing
other forms of slavery : he on his part challenged the
enslavement of captives, but proceeded to theorise that
some were slaves by " nature " in respect of their need
to be governed, their unfitness for self-government.[2]
But as soon as he goes into detail he is forced to acknowledge that such need and unfitness are universal, merely
varying in degree,[3] so that his appeal to " nature " is
quashed ; and when he proceeds to treat the problem of
practical management he simply suppresses the ethical
challenge which his own admissions invite, taking it for
granted that " the members of every well-regulated state
should be free from servile labour," but admitting that
nobody had yet hit on the proper way of managing
slaves, since these everywhere tend to be insubordinate.[4]
That a great political thinker could avow this, and yet
not see the explanation in the anti-social character of

[1] See the *Politics*, i. 3, 5, 6. [2] *Id.*, i. 2, 6.
[3] *Id.*, i. 13. [4] *Id.*, ii. 9.

slavery, is to be explained only by regarding him as standing wilfully to his acquired bias, his social habit.

When this is realised, we have gone some way towards solving the utilitarian problem : Had there not been slavery in the ancient world, how would civilisation have gone ? In one aspect the question is quite idle, for slavery was the outcome of the total ethical, political, and economic life ; and to suppose a social evolution without slavery is to suppose *all* these conditions different. But for this very reason, you will see, it is idle to argue that slavery was a good thing inasmuch as it promoted civilisation. To have done without it, say in Greece, men in general must have been better, juster, wiser, nobler ; and such nobler men could well have evolved a higher civilisation than was actually produced. They could have provided variously for the leisure of their students, and so have escaped the pernicious idleness which actually injured Greek city life ; and they might have made their polity permanent. And inasmuch as some men strove to persuade the others to renounce the evil thing, they were as truly right, and their opponents as truly wrong, as men ever are in any strife of ideals.

Slavery was as certainly a means of social corruption and dissolution as it was a means to the existence of a leisured class : Aristotle's admissions say as much ; and those who opposed it were, as we can now see, on the line of social preservation. This is the specifically sociological side of the case. They were further more sympathetic, more self-critical, more sincere in this regard than the champions of use and wont. This is the specifically moral side of the case. To say, then, that slavery was " not wrong " is to make the words right and wrong meaningless. It may indeed be plausibly argued that *both* terms are in such a case inapplicable ; that a wrong act is that which is seen to be such in terms of the recognised ethic of an age ; and that Greek slavery was not so regarded, since even the slaves themselves, if freed, would readily have enslaved others. But on this view the thesis that ancient slavery was *right* is already disposed of ; and for the rest, to argue that it was " neither right nor wrong " because most people did not see it to be wrong is to confuse the issue as to what constitutes wrongness. We all agree—all non-burglars, I mean—that objectively a burglary is wrong even if the burglar holds that he is as justifiably employed as a trader. His cast of mind is a reason for not seeking to make him suffer more than is involved in protecting society from him ; but we must all the same class his act as anti-social. It is not by counting the number of people for and against a given course that we can decide whether it is right or wrong : a majority vote proves at most that the course in question is permitted by the majority. But if we are convinced that the majority in so deciding is inconsistent and unjust ; that it is trampling down a minority's " rights " ; that it is not doing as it would be done by, and is passionately ignoring the fact, then we who are not of the majority will rationally pronounce its action to be wrong.

Certainly it is not of much importance to insist that ancient slavery was wrong when nobody is saying the contrary ; but when some do, as aforesaid, say the contrary, we are near to a vital moral issue. For the only practical purpose of such an assertion is to induce us to do otherwise than we would be done by in our own day, on the plea that in so doing we may advance civilisation. This plea we have now partly considered ; but we must consider it further. The preliminary answer is that all such calculations are in the first place grossly inconsistent, since they never admit the notion that *we* on the same score ought not to resent a felt " wrong " done to *us*, and in the second place grossly fallacious because they never take into account the reactions of the course proposed. I might put the matter more briefly by saying that such arguments are the negation of all morality, since morality actually consists in a code held to be reciprocally binding. This is clear enough to all, I suppose, when an individual goes about to square his conduct on the assumption either that his gain should be his sole moral criterion, or that his gain must in the end be a gain to civilisation. In the social relation we positively must have reciprocity if we are to have continuance. If a man lies to us or cheats or robs us, we shall not be induced to tolerate his acts by any hypothesis on his part that his lying and cheating furthers civilisation by helping him to live.

Eugene Aram, of famous memory, is said to have reasoned that he might fitly commit a murder in order to turn to the promotion of his useful studies money which its owner would not have put to any good account. He was reasoning exactly as do those theorists who say we may fitly overthrow by violence a backward State in order to hasten the development of its civilisation. Well, the rational answer to Eugene Aram (apart from the fact of the danger he incurred) would have been, firstly, that he could *not* know that his possession of the money would benefit mankind : he could only guess that it would ; secondly, that the same argument would, on his own showing, entitle anybody to murder him ; and, thirdly, that he had entirely overlooked the question of the possible moral reaction of his act upon himself. A great psychological novelist of our day, Dostoyevsky, has wonderfully imagined a case of the kind, in which a needy student, mentally shaken by hardship, kills a greedy old woman, thinking to rid the world of a worthless being and turn her money to his own good purposes. He is, however, morally paralysed by the unforeseen horror of his own act, and lives in a mere trance of new suffering until he gives himself up to the police. Now, it is not to be assumed that this is what would happen in every case of a crime so motived ; but the mere recognition of the possibility is enough to withhold any sane man from such a deed. On the other hand, it is obvious that no such proof can ever conceivably be given of good results from private murder and robbery as could induce a community to dream of applauding them.

All this, I say, is obvious enough : no one argues otherwise. But, as I have remarked, it is not uncommon at present to find men arguing that as between communities the moral principle of reciprocity does not hold ; that a State *may* be justified in international burglary and what we may term political garotting on a mere calculation of probable gain to future humanity from its act. A given community, they say,[1] is backward, ignorant, and conservative : let us conquer it, no matter at what cost of slaughter and devastation, and of cruelty to non-combatants, seeing that when the bloodshed is

[1] China is sometimes pointed to in my day. I wonder how *that* case will have gone in yours.

over a new generation will reap an abundant profit in improved conditions. We have here a reversion, within certain limits, to an old species of doctrine, commonly but dubiously fathered on the Jesuits as a body—the doctrine that the end justifies the means. And some men give the doctrine a superficially fresh aspect by identifying it with Utilitarianism.

Now, there have been committed many oversights of argument in the name of Utilitarianism, as in the name of every other principle; but no reasoning can get away from the central facts that *all* moral systems assume the ultimate coincidence of utility with right action; and that men in the long run are persuaded to act on any code only in the belief that it is useful either to themselves or to others. We must then be ready to meet rationally any such attempt as that under notice, to prove that a course repulsive to our developed notions of goodness and righteousness is in reality useful to humanity. I have personally a good deal of sympathy with " Intuitionists " who resent and denounce such attempts to carry back all acquired moral notions to a calculation of consequences. The charm and the profit of association with good people lie largely in the very fact that as regards most things they have evolved past such calculation; that they never dream of calculating whether it will " pay " them to be just, or straightforward, or kind, or courageous; and I do not think that even one who falls short of that spontaneity of goodness—unless he fall very far short of it indeed— ever admires others of his kind, or fails to admire in his heart those who attain it. A man who should either profess or seem to calculate in every case whether honesty is the best policy, or whether he will gain by speaking the truth, would, I fancy, establish in us a tolerably deep distrust.

The historical and psychological fact is that certain habits of reciprocity have come to be normal and " instinctive " with at least a large number of us, so that, though in the case of certain lines of action we admit and apply the test of utility, the " ethic of consequences," in respect of these established habits we recoil from the suggestion of any resort to such a test. Such questions as those of the fitness of indissoluble or official marriage, the secularisation of Sunday, the payment of certain taxes, and many other matters of politics, must be tried by the test of utility, which, by the way, is no simple matter. Those who affect to settle them by appeals either to authority or to instinct are moralists to whom we need pay little attention. It is otherwise with the case of a person who invites us to join him in a safe fraud, or in an act of physical or moral cruelty : there most of us feel disgust that the utility of such courses should still be thought to be arguable. And I confess to feeling some such disgust when I am asked to believe that the members of a community may usefully further civilisation by wantonly doing to another community what they would passionately resent having done to their own. When, however, the intuitionist declares (if, indeed, he does so express himself : at times he appears to be intuitionally on the side of the pseudo-utilitarians) that he " feels " such an act is wrong, and that nothing will induce him to be a party to it, he sets us reflecting on the fact that men have as avowedly and as obviously " felt " the rightness of many acts that to us now seem hideous wrongs—such as the slaying of heretics, the enslavement of captives and their children, the selling away of slaves' wives and families, the torturing of witnesses, the flogging of madmen, the special degradation of women for acts in which they were partners with unpunished men, and a hundred others of the long list of instituted social iniquities. This (to the study of which I shall return) is the fatal weakness of professedly " intuitional " morality. While one intuitionist may see that a given act is a breach of the law of reciprocity, and as such man denounce it, another, too prejudiced or self-interested to see as much, may " feel " that the act is perfectly righteous.

No doubt the intuitionist (or, as he might be more fitly termed, the Apriorist) may insist that the law of reciprocity, the obligation to do as we would be done by, is absolute, and may argue that this is not denied by the opposing intuitionist, who claims that he *is* doing as he would be done by. But we have noted that the law of reciprocity has to be defined as between individuals ; and the process of definition is inevitably an appeal to utilitarian tests. Let us not then, I repeat, hesitate to meet any challenge to define it as between communities. For my own part I am satisfied, with Mr. Spencer, that the so-called instinct of reciprocity as between individuals emerges most often as a one-sided sense of our own rights, and that only by pressures of external criticism and of the reflection which comes after experience does it take a properly balanced shape. Mr. Spencer puts it that the " sentiment " of justice comes before the " idea " of justice : meaning by the former our sense of our own rights, and by the latter our recognition of the correlation of other people's. It would be better, I think, to say simply that a self-regarding idea *or* sentiment of justice usually precedes an other-regarding one ; but, terminology apart, the proposition seems to me essentially true. And if it be so, it need not be surprising to us that, in the relations of communities, the idea or sentiment of other-regarding justice should lag far behind the earlier and simpler notion.

In the case of individuals, I do not doubt, the full sense of the force of the law of reciprocity is partly built up by experiences and calculations of utility. I think I can see this in the case of you two children from day to day ; and I think I can in a measure trace the process even in my own adult experience, to say nothing of my youthful recollections. Most if not all of us tend to be inconsiderate in a hundred ways ; and a sense of the charm and benefit of another's considerateness, or the shock of another's want of it, in a given case, is really an educative perception of the utility of such considerateness. It is conceivable that even a perception of the utility of honesty and candour may set up a choice in favour of honesty and candour on the part of one not strongly predisposed to them. If this were not so, human prospects would be darker than they are. I should indeed have no great hope of converting to my own inclination anyone who argues that we ought to disavow or conceal all unpopular opinions for the sake of our comfort or our incomes. Such a reasoner I should take to be devoid of the *bias* which involves (*a*) the finding of a satisfaction (= utility) in standing for an unpopular truth even unsuccessfully, and further involves (*b*) pain at the thought of having turned one's back on it for ease or gain. But I can conceive that even one without this bias may by early education, early instruction as to the ultimate social utilities of straightforwardness, be prepared to take the braver and better course, even as one not naturally much endowed with considerateness may be educated by others so endowed to act more sympathetically than he otherwise would. It may not be quite unprofitable, then, to prove that moral reciprocity is the best policy as between nation and nation.

To begin with, much reasoning on the subject is false by reason of the loose or illogical use of terms. The one word "civilisation," in the hands of prejudiced or superficial people, is made to play many tricks. Implicitly assuming that civilisation is always better than incivilisation, they reason that any process which sets up the material phenomena of civilisation in a given place or race where before they were lacking is an unquestionable gain to mankind. Applying an ostensibly utilitarian test, they do not attempt any utilitarian analysis. They do not ask whether the change adds to average happiness, or whether, supposing it to make some people happier, it does not relatively impoverish and degrade others. Yet it is almost a commonplace of practical sociology that myriads of people in civilised cities exist in worse life conditions than those of an average savage.

The same reasoners are apt to take it for granted that civilisation by way of conquest is just as good a thing as civilisation by way of peaceful contact and progress, and that because in past history conquest has entered into the development of most nations it either must or profitably may be deliberately practised in future in many if not in all cases. They never ask (any more than do the pro-slavery moralists in regard to ancient slavery) how civilisation would or might have gone in the past if men could have been educated to abstain from conquest on principle. Now, a careful study of history will reveal to you that *all* the civilisations of antiquity underwent decadence ; that this decadence is always associated with both the infliction and the suffering of conquest ; and that it was precisely where civilisation was most advanced—where men had become in the largest proportion of cases capable of reasoning on the morality of it—that the fatality is plainest.

At the stage at which men practise conquest most instinctively, with least pretence of having philanthropic reasons, with the most spontaneous belief that " he should take who has the power "—then it is that conquest is most often compatible with gain to civilisation. It is when, having become capable of realising that conquest is the doing as we would not be done by, they brazen out the act with insincere Virgilian formulas, that it is seen, intelligibly enough, to work their own swift demoralisation. That which for primitive man is an unreflecting animal activity is for more developed man a lawless act. Modern Europeans turned pirates are much lower types than ancient Greeks who never were anything else. So with nations which revert to the spirit of tribal savagery. They have repudiated the normal basis of their reasoned ethic ; and the result is domestic as well as international. Give up the law of reciprocity as between States, and you are already inclined to give it up as between diverging groups within the State : cancel it as between them, and you are prepared to annul it as between individuals. And this actually happened in antiquity again and again. Read the history of Rome from the conquest of Carthage to the end of the Republic, and you will get the most fully documented case.

Consider next this, that of all the so-called barbarian or semi-civilised States effectually overrun by Rome, not one was made capable of maintaining itself when the central part of the empire gave way, and you will partly realise how vain a thing is a forcibly imposed civilisation. But that, after all, is a less impressive thought than the perception that for any State to set up the pretension of being the forcible civiliser of others is to set up in every other, in the degree of its knowledge, the spirit not only of hostility, but of a hostility which feels that towards such a threatening force it need not be scrupulous. The State which collectively harbours the thesis that *it* may fitly decline to do as it would be done by has justified every other State in planning its overthrow. To justify us in supposing that any State can thrive by avowing its readiness to do as it would not be done by, we should need evidence that a community any more than a man can permanently thrive by the ill-will of neighbours. Was such evidence ever forthcoming ?

Were it not that I am seeking rather to make you reasoners than to furnish you with historical demonstrations, I could add much to similar effect ; but I have said enough to indicate to you how thoughtless, how ill-reasoning, are many of those who undertake to give rational grounds for deeds which outrage the developed sense and the normal standard of righteousness. They profess to estimate future utilities, a thing that could be rationally done only after the closest study of past utilities ; and they make no calculation whatever, falling back on verbal formulas which beg the question. They are, in fact, playing fast and loose with reason while professing to stand or fall by its light. And to realise this is in a measure to realise that you need not be afraid to let rational tests be put to any of your moral convictions. Observe, you may happen to have moral convictions which will not stand rational tests. If you had been brought up, for instance, to believe in Sabbath observance, and had been challenged to explain rationally why one should object to play any game on a Sunday, you could not do so : you must fall back on dogma or admit that you held to mere habit. If, again, you were trained to think your own country must have been in the right in every one of its wars, and were searchingly questioned by one who knew better, your " feeling " would not save you from argumentative discomfiture. And the only way to make sure that any of your moral positions is not thus arbitrary is just to test it when it is challenged. But it would be disturbing to feel that the " instincts " on which you speak the truth to your fellows and render good for good might in some particular instance be open to repudiation ; and I advise you to reach moral security once for all by testing every pretence to that effect. I venture to promise you that you will find them as unsatisfactory to the head as to the heart.

There is indeed one stock case of opportunist ethics which seems to give some people trouble. By the time you read these letters you will probably have heard of the problem whether we can ever be justified in telling an untruth. Some argue that it is always unjustifiable : many, on the contrary, are satisfied that if by telling an untruth to a would-be murderer—say in the case of his asking us which way a fugitive had gone—we can prevent a crime, we ought to tell it ; and that if by deceiving a sick person we can save a life, or if by withholding a horrible truth in some special circumstances we can save some innocent person intense moral suffering, we ought so to suppress the truth. Most reasoning men, I think, take the latter view ; but the philosopher Kant insisted on the former. He argued that if you see a man with a weapon running after another who has passed near you, and the pursuer should ask you which way the fugitive went, you are morally bound either to refuse to tell him anything, or to tell him the truth. If a murder should result, says Kant, you are then not responsible ; whereas if you should chance, by telling an untruth, unexpectedly to enable the murderer to overtake the fugitive in the case of the latter having changed his course after he has passed you, you would be guilty of facilitating the murder.

Let us argue the case out. We may simplify the problem at once by supposing that the pursuer asks us such a question (as " Did a man run *that* way ? ") that if we refuse to answer it he will readily infer the truth. And we may considerably strengthen Kant's rather flimsy case by raising the hypothesis that for all we know the flying man may be a dangerous criminal or madman, and that the pursuer is carrying a weapon not for slaughter but for self-defence. How is such a problem to be solved ?

I answer, by utilitarian tests, and by them only. Let us first put a somewhat different case—that of an obvious madman who is threatening our life. There is a story that a madman who had got to the top of London Monument said to a sane man whom he found there : " I am able to throw you down to the street, and I am going to do it " ; whereupon the sane man coolly replied : " Oh, that is nothing : I could throw you up here from below, which is a far harder thing." The madman, in the story, consented to go down to have the experiment tried, whereupon he was secured by the police. Now, I fancy that even Kant would in that case condone the untruth. If he refused, I should simply waive further argument, taking as my ultimate position the primary right of self-defence, and affirming that my right to deceive the madman in self-defence is as clear as my right to resist him if he tries to kill me.

Kant, I suppose, would have assented in this case on the score that a madman is as such incapable of normal moral relations; that he must be regarded as for the time being in the relation of a wild animal to us. Well, exactly on that ground I should justify the act of deceiving the man apparently bent on murder. In the case put, we might and indeed should in reason question the questioner, in order to gather if possible whether he was or was not bent on murder; and if we were satisfied that he was, it would be our clear social duty (if we recognised any such duty) to deceive in order to baffle him, as a person making war on the social system. I suppose Kant would admit our right to resist the would-be slayer if in our presence he sought to commit murder, though in so resisting him we might do him severe bodily injury. To say that we are justified in breaking his head, but not in deceiving him, seems to me a rather gross absurdity. If, on the other hand, our attempt to deceive him should by mischance really lead him in the path the fugitive had actually taken, and so facilitate his crime, we should indeed be bitterly grieved; but as we had done our very best, in our view of the circumstances, to prevent it, we should certainly not be guilty. If, on the contrary, we had facilitated the act either by telling the truth or by maintaining a silence from which the murderer inferred the truth, we might well reproach ourselves bitterly, inasmuch as we had *not* striven to prevent the crime, and had sacrificed good to the form of good, the spirit to the letter. Thus to separate the formula of right from all consideration of moral consequences is to put the very essentials of morals in jeopardy by leaving it without rational sanctions.

Kant, perhaps, would argue further that by telling an untruth in any one case we weaken our moral nature. I should answer that we certainly do so if we transgress the normal law of reciprocity and deceive for mere gain or personal convenience; but that in the case put we

no more vitiate our sense of truth than we brutalise
ourselves when in an emergency we use violence to save
a friend from worse violence. If, for instance, I saw
either of you attacked by a vicious dog, and in order
to save you beat or even killed the dog, I should be
at least suffering less moral deterioration than I should
undergo by standing by and doing nothing ; and it
really need not follow that I should develop a proclivity
to killing dogs.

So far, on the other hand, is Kant's moral fanaticism
from safeguarding the moral sense that we actually find
him, the absolutist, the professed ascetic of veracity,
grossly transgressing his own law where there is hardly
a shadow of excuse for it. It might seem incredible, but
it is the fact, that he who pronounced it unjustifiable
to deceive a would-be murderer in order to save a life,
expressly condoned the utterance by a priest of a religious doctrine in which he does not believe—this on
the score that " populus vult decipi," and that the priest
cannot help himself.[1] I know no stranger anomaly in
the literature of ethics ; and I do not see how we can
escape the conclusion that Kant was in this connection
profoundly " insincere." He seems to have framed his
argument against deceiving the armed pursuer in order
to buttress a formula he had already espoused, knowing
that there was small risk of having his doctrine put to
the test in his daily walk in the avenue of Königsberg.
But where his own convenience, or that of many of
his disciples, was seriously imperilled by the command
to speak the truth and shame the devil, he virtually
gave them and himself *carte blanche* where you and I,
I hope, would refuse to accept it.

Let us take that case in turn on its merits. It is the
fate of many men to be committed to an ecclesiastical
career in youth, before they can rightly judge of the
truth of the creed they are taught, and to find themselves in later years painfully convinced of its untruth,
yet unable to abandon their clerical vocation without
putting in danger of extreme hardship those who are

[1] *Religion innerhalb der Grenzen der blossen Vernunft*, B. III.
Apotome i. sect. 6 ; B. IV. Apot. ii., preamble and sect. i. 3, 4.
Cp. the comment of Baur, *Kirchengeschichte des 19ten Jahrh.*, 1862,
p. 65.

dearest to them, and for whose well-being they are responsible. For men so placed I have nothing but sympathy ; and so long as they have the sincerity to abstain from maligning or belittling those who are free to and do avow heretical opinions, I should never dream of disparaging them. Economic pressure in our ill-framed society is too ubiquitous and too powerful a force to be fairly regarded as morally negligible. My honoured friend, the late Charles Bradlaugh, was in the course of his life privately consulted by quite a number of clergymen so placed, and his habit was to urge on the single men that they should take their fortunes in their hands and give up their posts at any risk, but to tell the married ones that their first duty lay in providing for their wives and children, and to warn them that it might be very difficult to do so if they cut adrift from their office and sought to earn a living as simple teachers of the truth.

Thus did a wise utilitarian reason, who in his own case had always made truth the first consideration, and had throughout life unflinchingly faced the endless penalties incurred by those who steadfastly impugn popular error. But the transcendentalist, the preacher of uncompromising veracity, is found not merely commuting his commandment on the slightest pressure of his personal interest, but virtually encouraging the disillusioned priest to persist in make-believe when he might without injury to others or even to himself renounce his false position and take one where he could preach truth with no other hindrance than that which comes of popular prejudice.

It is not now necessary, I hope, to remind you that by the utilitarian test Kant's counsel is as indefensible in this case as his veto was in the other. The deliberate resort to make-believe in religion *does* work moral evil in a hundred ways. Men often guess, indeed, that evil-doers are to be restrained by threatening them with hell-fire and bribing them with the proffer of vicarious salvation ; when they might ascertain by enquiry that the vast majority of criminals have always been believers in such religious doctrines, and that on the other hand the deliberate and calculated practice of deception, under no coercion of a grave need, does corrupt the men who resort to it.   But such are the incongruities of human nature that you are likely to meet in your lives with many moralists who on the one hand profess to repudiate the morality of consequences, and on the other justify by utilitarian pleas courses which you would be ashamed to take.

I have heard such a moralist, a man of culture and apparent moral earnestness, denounce as demoralising the " naturalistic " view of human actions, and in the same discourse bitterly reproach rationalists for saying that we should always seek and teach the truth for its own sake.   " Would you," he asked, " insist on telling an innocent child of the wickedness of his mother ? " That is exactly what a moral-minded utilitarian would not do ; and the pretence that the demand for true teaching about religion is on a par with such an act is itself an act of sheer moral baseness.   By " teach the truth " we mean " let that which you teach be truth," and it does not even imply that a true doctrine is to be forced on people who do not want to listen to it. To such basenesses of misrepresentation, however, men frequently resort in their determination to defend their beliefs anyhow ; and I warn you on the one hand to be prepared for such basenesses in your intercourse with men, and on the other to be anxiously on your guard lest you should ever descend to similar courses.   Let your loyalty to your ostensible " intuitions " be such as to preserve you from the unworthy devices of dialectic to which professed intuitionists so often descend, and which are so poorly justified by what Mr. Spencer calls " the profoundest of all infidelity—the fear lest the truth should be bad "—bad, that is, for mankind in mass and in perpetuity.

I have now, I hope, made clear to you how it is that on one hand I hold good instincts to be the root of right action, and the complete lack of them to be incurable by any sort of moral doctrine, though a moderate endowment of them may be much improved upon by rational appeals ; while on the other hand I repeat that a reference to moral instinct as a standard independent of all utilitarian tests is futile from the point of view of moral persuasion, and is as readily resorted to in a bad cause as in a good.   In point of fact, almost none of those who profess to hold by such a standard do really adhere to it. I referred above to the late Dr. Martineau's declaration that a substitution of a utilitarian for an intuitionist ethic makes a complete change in our moral dynamics. This, you will see on reflection, is really a utilitarian argument, an appeal to the test of consequences in the very act of repudiating such a test. " If you become a utilitarian," says Dr. Martineau in effect, " you will become a worse man." I have tried to show you how what is really moral in Dr. Martineau's recoil from rationalistic methods is perfectly preserved when you take the step he is afraid to take. He was somewhat in the position of the Paduan professor described by Galileo, who resolutely refused to look through Galileo's telescope at those satellites of Jupiter in which he declined to believe. Your loyalty to the evolved higher " instincts " is not, I think, impaired by the demonstration that they really make for the welfare of mankind ; and the recognition of this fact will one day, I think, make an end of the strife between so-called intuitionalism and utilitarianism.

INDEX